Ken Thomas

D0457627

☞ THE   NEGOTIATING   GAME ☜

CHESTER L. KARRASS

THE NEGOTIATING GAME

THE WORLD PUBLISHING COMPANY

NEW YORK AND CLEVELAND

PUBLISHED BY THE WORLD PUBLISHING COMPANY
2231 West 110th Street, Cleveland, Ohio 44102

Published simultaneously in Canada by Nelson, Foster & Scott Ltd.

FIRST PRINTING—1970

Library of Congress Catalog Card Number: 70-108197

PRINTED IN THE UNITED STATES OF AMERICA

WORLD PUBLISHING
TIMES MIRROR

This book is dedicated to my wife, Virginia, and our teenage negotiators, Lynn and Gary, with whom we occasionally deadlock.

CONTENTS

LIST OF ILLUSTRATIONS

LIST OF TABLES

INTRODUCTION

Despite the fact that man has stepped on the moon and harnessed the atom, he is still bargaining as he did in ancient times. If a five-thousand-year-old Babylonian were to dress in a business suit and sit opposite us at the table, there is little reason to believe his methods would differ from ours. It is as though time stood still; as though the written word, the printing press, management and the scientific method had never been invented.

Incredible as it may seem, this is the first book to integrate modern analytical thinking with good practice at the bargaining table. It is the product of almost twenty years experience as a negotiator and three years of intensive research. The logical methods developed are as applicable to lawyers and diplomats as they are to buyers and sellers.

Negotiation is too serious a business to be treated superficially. This book will not guarantee that you will achieve success by following a list of do's and don'ts. I have yet to meet the experienced negotiator who attaches any importance to such a list. In this book the subject is treated in a mature and modern way. There is, after all, an explosion of new ideas in every field. Why not negotiation?

The book is divided into three parts. The first deals with a large experiment involving professional negotiators. This study sought to discover how skilled men achieved their objectives not only when they had power but when they did not. The second part looks at the heart of negotiation by exposing to your view elements such as power and aspiration level. These basic building blocks of bargaining, if understood, can spell the difference between good and mediocre performance. The third part is concerned with the practical realities of negotiating to win—through better strategy, tactics and organization.

This work is founded on the assumption that men who negotiate know a good deal about their own business. They know how to buy, how to write an airtight clause, how to make a sale and how to conduct diplomacy. If they do not, this is hardly the place to learn. I am assuming that it is negotiation, not cost-analysis or legal doctrine, about which the reader wants to know more. There is, therefore, one emphasis only; and that is, to provide a practical method by which men can negotiate more effectively to win their objectives.

PART I

New

Frontiers

in

Negotiation

CHAPTER 1

THE
NEGOTIATING
SOCIETY

AFTER AN ERA OF CONFRONTATION, THE TIME HAS
COME FOR AN ERA OF NEGOTIATION.

Richard M. Nixon

MANY OF THE PATTERNS AND PROCESSES WHICH CHARAC-
TERIZE CONFLICT IN ONE AREA ALSO CHARACTERIZE IT IN
OTHERS. NEGOTIATION AND MEDIATION GO ON IN LABOR
DISPUTES AS WELL AS IN INTERNATIONAL RELATIONS. PRICE
WARS AND DOMESTIC QUARRELS HAVE MUCH THE PATTERN
OF AN ARMS RACE.

Journal of Conflict Resolution

Once upon a time there was a bear who was hungry and a
man who was cold, so they decided to negotiate in a neutral
cave. After several hours a settlement was reached. When they
emerged the man had a fur coat and the bear was no longer
hungry.

In life it is just as hard to determine whether the outcome
of a negotiation favors one party or the other. It is said that in
a successful negotiation everybody wins. Let us be realistic.

In a successful negotiation both parties gain, but more often than not one party wins more than the other. In this book we will find out why some people win and others lose; and why losers make substantially larger concessions than necessary while winners do not.

The potential for negotiation exists whenever men buy and sell. Terms of sale may be open to discussion even when price is not. For example, a purchasing executive whom I know recently bought a new house in a wealthy development. When he tried to negotiate price, he found the developer firm. After moving in he learned that a neighbor had obtained better credit terms. Despite long and successful experience in purchasing, it simply had not occurred to him that credit terms were flexible in such a transaction.

Negotiation plays a subtle part in everyday affairs. At work we *bargain* with supervision for high stakes. Those successful win a greater share of money, freedom and respect. Some capable men are always told precisely what to do while others are treated as thinking human beings. Some quiver at the sight of authority while others hold their heads high and demand a share of power. Some managers get work done by force while others exert influence through persuasion, loyalty and reason. A negotiation takes place whenever ideas are exchanged for the purpose of influencing behavior.

It is said that a camel is a horse designed by a committee. The Edsel was a manmade camel designed by negotiating executives at the Ford Motor Company. Those who said it would not sell did not prevail and a half-billion dollars was lost. When executives meet to make decisions they represent differing points of view and aspiration levels. The outcome, as in all bargaining, is based upon power and bargaining skill as well as logic. It is well to remember that budgets and schedules represent *negotiated* decisions between men who have *joint and conflicting interests.*

Congress allocates funds for highways, construction

projects and water programs. There is no *Golden Rule* that
specifies what is or is not fair; no simple formula determines
what share belongs to Idaho, Texas or California. Justice notwithstanding, the allocation of federal funds is settled by hard
bargaining. In 1968 I read that a young Western Senator told
a reporter that he did not "give a damn" for President Johnson's Vietnam policy. The President reportedly retorted, "That
guy will give a damn when he tries to get a dam." Later in
the chapter we will learn of a politician who was probably
the *worst* negotiator of his time, and perhaps of all time.

Ninety percent of all lawsuits are settled out of court.
Some lawyers have high aspirations and thereby enrich their
clients; others do not. One lawyer may believe that a whip-
lash case is worth $3,000 while another may appraise the same
case at $5,000. The critical role of bargaining skill and aspira-
tion level in determining settlement outcome will receive
detailed attention later.

Some businessmen are poor negotiators. They unknow-
ingly give away the store. The story that follows involves the
loss of a relatively large amount of money in only a *few hours*.
Because it is true, the company name has been changed to
protect those who still work there.

THE STARMATIC COMPANY

Years ago the aerospace industry was a lot better off
than it is today. When the Russians began the "space race"
with Sputnik in 1957, Americans were shocked. They realized
that President Eisenhower had made a poor decision in
scrapping space supremacy for economic reasons.

After Sputnik the people demanded action. This was good
news for those in the missile business. Since few suppliers
knew anything about this new technology, the government
was willing to spend money to teach them. Study contracts

were given to anyone who could spell "elliptical orbit."
President Kennedy, shortly after his inauguration, challenged
the Russians to a "moon race," thereby committing us for a
decade.

In 1961 the Hughes Aircraft Company received a large
contract to land the first unmanned space vehicle on the moon.
Since this had never before been tried, the contract was placed
on a cost-plus-fixed-fee basis. This meant that the company
would earn a fixed profit whether actual costs were 50, 100
or 500 million dollars. In theory a company has nothing to
gain by running costs up unnecessarily but may use a certain
amount of discretion in developing advanced designs. Spending
and technical progress is monitored by the government on a
continual basis.

Two years later design engineers decided to purchase
special power-generating equipment for the spacecraft. A bid
specification was written and submitted to four companies,
one of which responded. Starmatic Company bid $450,000 on
a firm fixed-price basis. The company had considerable experience producing less complex generating equipment.

For one month after the proposal was received, a series
of major spacecraft changes occurred that required design
re-evaluation. During that time the purchasing cost-analysts
were busy on other contracts and paid no attention to Starmatic's proposal. As it turned out this was a dangerous over-
sight, for a management decision was made to award the
contract to Starmatic and begin negotiations immediately. I
was part of a three-man group assembled at 9:00 A.M. and
told to complete contract arrangements that day. There are
occasions in this business when time is so important that
savings in negotiation are more than offset by production-
delay costs. This was such a case.

An early afternoon meeting was arranged at the supplier's
plant. Three decisions were made enroute to the conference:
to be stubborn; to settle for $425,000 if possible; and to offer

$140,000 initially. This was the full extent of our foolish planning.

We soon learned that the opponent's team was in greater disarray than our own. Their chief engineer was *not* conversant with the original proposal and felt obliged to apologize for his lack of detailed knowledge. The supplier's contract administrator and controller indicated that they had not reviewed the proposal prior to the conference and asked for a short delay in order to do so.

We requested accounting justification for the $450,000 bid and were pleased that the controller lacked this. He left the room and returned almost thirty minutes later with an *armful of messy workpapers.*

We continued to insist upon accounting justification and began to realize that the estimating base was not likely to be found in the books. Starmatic's cost system was no better than that of the rest of the industry.

As bargaining went on the chief engineer left the room several times in order to be present during critical acceptance tests. It was apparent that he preferred to solve technical problems rather than discuss price. The contract man was also interrupted a number of times with urgent questions from subordinates relating to other proposal work being done.

Late that afternoon Starmatic had reduced its price to $375,000. By mid-evening they further reduced it to $300,000. The contract was settled at midnight for $220,000. *Both parties were pleased.* To the best of my knowledge Starmatic suffered no loss on the job, but will never know that they threw away over $200,000 at the table. The Starmatic negotiators *aspired to little; little is what they got.**

---

* On June 2, 1966, *Surveyor,* designed and developed by the Hughes Aircraft Company, made a perfect soft landing on the moon. It was the first unmanned space vehicle to perform such a difficult feat and paved the way for man's exploration of the planets. The work was accomplished within a small percentage of estimated cost and substantially on schedule.

THE RAPE OF CZECHOSLOVAKIA

The inability to bargain effectively can result in consequences far beyond the mere loss of money. In 1938, Prime Minister Chamberlain did an incredibly poor job at Munich. For three years Hitler had taken spectacular gambles and won. Against the advice of his generals, he had rearmed the country, rebuilt the navy and established a powerful air force. Hitler correctly sensed that the British and French wanted peace desperately, for they had chosen to overlook German rearmament and expansionism. Encouraged by success, Germany applied pressure on Austria and occupied the country early in 1938. Czechoslovakia was next.

Hitler was not fully satisfied with earlier victories, as they had been bloodless. He yearned to show the world how powerful Germany was by provoking a shooting war, and he did this by making impossibly high demands on the Czech Government for German minority rights and by establishing an October 1, 1938, war deadline. It was a ridiculous gamble.

As shown in Table 1, relative bargaining strength was *overwhelmingly* in favor of the Allies on September 27, 1938.[1] Hitler was aware of his weakness and chose to win by negotiation what could not be won by war. The following events indicate why he was optimistic:

1. On September 13, Chamberlain announced a willingness to grant large concessions if Hitler would agree to discuss issues.

2. On September 15 the aged Prime Minister of Great Britain made a grueling journey to meet Hitler deep in eastern Germany. Hitler had refused to meet him halfway.

3. Hitler opened the conference by abusing Chamberlain and by making outrageously large demands for territory, to which the leader of the Western world *immediately agreed.*

4. Hitler was aware that Chamblerlain spent the next four days convincing the French that Germany could be trusted. The Czechs were bluntly told not to be *unreasonable* by fighting back.

5. On September 22, Chamberlain flew back to eastern

GERMANY VS. ALLIES
RELATIVE BARGAINING STRENGTH. *Table 1*

THE GERMAN POSITION	THE ALLIED POSITION
1. German generals reported that the Czechs were determined to fight. They told Hitler that Czech fortifications were sufficiently strong to repulse the Germans even without military help from France and England.	1. A million Czechs were ready to fight from strong mountain fortresses.
2. German intelligence reported that French and Czech together outnumbered the Nazis two to one.	2. The French were prepared to place 100 divisions in the field.
3. The General Staff reported only twelve German divisions available to fight the French in the west.	3. Anti-Nazi generals in Germany were prepared to destroy Hitler if the Allies would commit themselves to resist the Czech takeover.
4. In Berlin a massive parade was staged. William L. Shirer reports that less than 200 Germans watched. Hitler attended and was infuriated by the lack of interest.	4. British and French public opinion was stiffening against Germany's outrageous demands.
5. German Intelligence reported that Mussolini had privately decided not to assist Hitler.	5. The British fleet, largest in the world, was fully mobilized for action.
6. German diplomats reported that world opinion was overwhelmingly pro-Czechoslovakian.	6. President Roosevelt pledged aid to the Allies.

Germany and offered Hitler *more* than he asked for. Hitler was astounded but nonplussed. *He raised his demands.*

6. Chamberlain returned home to argue Hitler's cause while the German leader made public announcements that war would start October 1 if his *moderate demands* were not granted.

When the two men met on September 29, Hitler had little doubt of victory. Mussolini acted as mediator (imagine that!) and proposed a small compromise, which was quickly accepted by both parties. And in a few months Czechoslovakia ceased to exist. Chamberlain, businessman turned politician, had lost the greatest negotiation of all time. As a consequence, 25 million people were soon to lose their lives.

WHO SHALL NEGOTIATE?

We have a right to know more about the men who represent us in international and business negotiations. Was the mortally ill Franklin D. Roosevelt the best choice at Yalta? Were Averell Harriman or Henry Cabot Lodge the best men for Paris? Does Roy Ash negotiate effectively when he purchases new companies for the Litton conglomerate? Does he pay far more for acquisitions than is necessary? In business as in diplomacy it may take years to recognize a poor agreement.

In choosing an attorney for a divorce or negligence case it may be wiser to select one who can bargain effectively than one deeply versed in legal technicalities. Most such cases do not involve complex legal issues. The business manager who represents an entertainer may not be a good negotiator even though he has the performer's best interest at heart. The agent may have too low a level of aspiration or too high a regard for those in power to bargain effectively.

President Nixon spoke of an "era of negotiation" in his acceptance speech. We enter such an era in all aspects of life from buying and selling to raising children. The children of tomorrow *must* be good negotiators. They must be prepared to resolve differences in a civilized way: to listen; to be responsive; and to be unafraid to adjust conflicting values. The alternative in an age of rising expectations is violence.

THE RIDDLE CALLED NEGOTIATION

Several years ago, after twenty years in industrial procurement and contracts, I was provided the opportunity through a Howard Hughes Doctoral Fellowship to pursue advanced studies at the University of Southern California. My dissertation consisted of a three-pronged attack on negotiation: analytical, experimental and opinion-sampling. Its goal was to answer the question "What determines the outcome of a negotiation?"

The purpose of thought is action. What follows in this book are practical ideas based on research. Leo Durocher, the feisty baseball manager, once said, "Nice guys don't win." I disagree. In negotiation, as in life, nice guys do win: They gain their objectives when they know what they are doing. It matters not if they are buyers, salesmen, politicians, lawyers or diplomats—or ballplayers. The principles are the same.

CHAPTER 2

WINNERS
AND
LOSERS

"FOR EXAMPLE" IS NO PROOF.

Proverb

WHAT AN INDIVIDUAL THINKS OR FEELS AS SUCCESS IS
UNIQUE TO HIM.

Alfred Adler

WHEN YOU CANNOT MEASURE IT, WHEN YOU CANNOT EX-
PRESS IT IN NUMBERS, YOUR KNOWLEDGE IS OF A MEAGER
AND UNSATISFACTORY KIND.

Lord Kelvin

The tale of Adam and Eve describes the first negotiation. We
have yet to learn the outcome of that exchange. Although men
have engaged in trade for over five thousand years, the
literature of negotiation contains almost nothing but anecdotes
and "home brewed" prescriptions of doubtful value. In today's
complex world, " *'for example' is no proof.*" We need something
more substantial than anecdotes. In the past few years a

handful of men have begun to adopt methods of disciplined logic and experimentation to this ancient profession.

When I first became seriously interested in negotiation I was intrigued by the paradox of power. I had seen buyers with little power confront sole-source suppliers with great vigor while other men under similar circumstances scraped and bowed. Many of us could not understand how Ho Chi Minh of Vietnam was willing to fight the United States. I began to wonder why some negotiators are intimidated by power while others are not.

Skill was another area of mystery. Most of the literature said that it was better to be skilled than unskilled. Many suggested that certain traits were essential to success. None suggested that it was possible to measure skill or evaluate the relative importance of one trait over another.

From experience it was easy to predict that skilled men would outperform those less skilled. Yet I could not help but wonder whether the difference in the amount of skill between opponents would affect the final outcome. I also wondered if it really mattered whether or not a negotiator with power was skilled. In my experience some very marginal buyers who held power had returned from conferences with good agreements.

The question of concession pattern was puzzling. Some professionals preferred to get right to the point while others compromised with reluctance, or not at all. Very little in the literature supported either viewpoint.

What emerged from all this was a series of questions that go to the heart of negotiation. Many had never before been tested. An experiment was designed to find answers of practical value. It was the first to explore the relationship between power, skill and outcome. It was also the first to use over one hundred professional buyers and sellers as experimental subjects and to measure their skill in objective terms.

These are the eight questions that the experiment sought to answer:

1. IS THERE A RELATIONSHIP BETWEEN ASPIRATION LEVEL AND SUCCESS?
2. DO WINNERS HAVE A DIFFERENT CONCESSION PATTERN THAN LOSERS?
3. IS POWER EXPLOITED DIFFERENTLY BY SKILLED AND UNSKILLED NEGOTIATORS?
4. DOES THE SKILL OF A NEGOTIATOR DETERMINE OUTCOME?
5. CAN SKILLED NEGOTIATORS ESTIMATE WHAT AN OPPONENT WANTS BETTER THAN THOSE LESS SKILLED?
6. IS SETTLEMENT TIME RELATED TO SUCCESS?
7. HOW ARE DEADLOCK, SUCCESS, AND FAILURE RELATED?
8. DO SUCCESSFUL AND UNSUCCESSFUL NEGOTIATORS REPORT EQUAL SATISFACTION WITH A FINAL AGREEMENT?

The most difficult part of the project was to design a method for measuring skill. It was somewhat easier to control power systematically, and to measure outcome and success in an objective way. How this was accomplished will be described briefly.*

THE METHOD

One hundred and twenty professional negotiators from four major aerospace companies volunteered to participate in the experiment. As buyers, subcontract administrators, contract managers and termination specialists, they represented the buying and selling side of the industry.

Each man was pre-evaluated by two of his managers

---

* For a detailed account of methodology the reader is directed to the dissertation "A Study of the Relationship of Negotiator Skill and Power as Determinants of Negotiation Outcome," Chester L. Karrass, University of Southern California, Los Angeles, California, 1968.

along a scale consisting of forty-five separate bargaining traits. Each trait was *individually weighted* on the basis of a survey of high-level purchasing executives. For example, the survey revealed that executives assigned a 15.0 weight to planning ability and a 1.2 weight to stamina. Neither managers nor volunteers were aware of the rating system or relative trait weights. Negotiator trait scores were determined by a computer.

Prior to the experiment all subjects were matched in sets according to trait score. Opponents met for the first time in a private office where they were given a plaintiff- or defense-attorney kit, which contained some information known to both

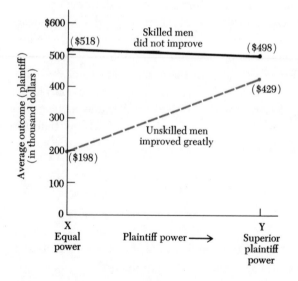

Figure 1. POWER AND NEGOTIATION OUTCOME

parties and some data of a private nature. Volunteers were provided thirty minutes to study the case, after which a bell rang commencing negotiation. If agreement was not reached within sixty minutes, the session was scored as a deadlock.

The bargaining involved a lawsuit between a drug company and a plaintiff who suffered damage to his eyes after taking a drug. The plaintiff sued for slightly more than a million dollars.

Two power variations were used. In the first the balance of power was approximately equal. In the second the power balance favored the plaintiff. In addition a small sample of *coached* unskilled defendants in the second group were induced to be aggressive in the face of their more powerful and skilled opponents. It was possible to create power imbalance simply by changing the number of precedent court decisions and by adding a degree of uncertainty to the equal-power variation.

The information obtained from the experiment included settlement amount, settlement time and concession history. In addition both parties were asked to record their own objectives and their estimates of the opponent's objectives. This information was recorded twice: at the beginning and midpoint of the negotiation. Twenty students and a university professor were on hand to answer questions and assure that forms were properly completed.

SUMMARY OF TERMS

The experimental results that follow can best be understood if a few basic terms are defined.

NEGOTIATOR TRAIT SCORE – *Manager rating of negotiator*

SKILLED NEGOTIATOR – *Negotiator whose trait score is above median*

UNSKILLED NEGOTIATOR	*– Negotiator whose trait score is below median*
SUCCESSFUL PLAINTIFF	*– A settlement above the plaintiff average*
SUCCESSFUL DEFENDANT	*– A settlement below the defendant average*
GAME "X"	*– Equal plaintiff and defendant power*
GAME "Y"	*– Plaintiff with superior power*

ASPIRATION LEVEL — RESULTS

QUESTION – Is there a relationship between aspiration level and success?

1. *FINDING* – PERSONS WITH HIGHER ASPIRATION LEVELS WON HIGHER AWARDS.*

This is probably the most important finding in the experiment. Winners started out wanting more and ended by getting more.

2. *FINDING* – SKILLED NEGOTIATORS WITH HIGH ASPIRATION LEVELS WERE BIG WINNERS REGARDLESS OF WHETHER THEY HAD POWER.*

One group won in almost every case: skilled negotiators with high aspirations. They were successful even when they had less power. A combination of ability and high aspirations appears to lead to success.

3. *FINDING* – PERSONS WITH HIGH ASPIRATIONS WERE WINNERS IN EVERY CASE WHERE THEY OPPOSED LOW ASPIRANTS.

* Wherever a finding is followed by an asterisk, it is to indicate that the level of significance is less than .05. Where the word "tend" is used in a finding, the level of significance is less than .10.

IT DID NOT MATTER WHETHER THEY WERE UNSKILLED OR HAD LESS POWER.*

When a man is lucky enough to face an opponent with low aspirations he is certain to win a great deal if he sets his goals high.

4. *FINDING* – THE MORE SKILLED THE NEGOTIATOR WITHOUT POWER, THE LOWER WAS HIS ASPIRATION LEVEL.*

Highly skilled men who lacked power became pessimistic and lowered their aspiration level. The unskilled who lacked power were more optimistic and *did not* reduce their aspirations. Perhaps they were more oblivious to reality.

CONCESSION BEHAVIOR—RESULTS

QUESTION – *Do winners have a different concession pattern than losers?*

1. *FINDING* – LARGE INITIAL DEMANDS IMPROVE THE PROBABILITY OF SUCCESS.*

It appears that those who give themselves room to compromise are more successful with people who open with a reasonable demand. Some students on American college campuses seem to have anticipated this finding. Certainly their demands are high enough. In one sense the backlash in various state capitals represents high demands in the other direction.

2. *FINDING* – LOSERS MAKE THE LARGEST CONCESSION IN A NEGOTIATION.*

Winners almost never made the largest single concession. Lawyers in particular may be interested in the fact that successful defendants did not make the largest concession in *any* negotiation.

3. *FINDING* – PEOPLE WHO MAKE SMALL CONCESSIONS DURING NEGOTIATIONS FAIL LESS.*

Those players who were obstinate—that is, those with low concession rates—rarely lost. They either deadlocked or won.

4. *FINDING* – LOSERS TEND TO MAKE THE FIRST COMPROMISE.

Successful bargainers force the opponent to offer the first concession. There were several deadlocks without a concession on either side.

5. *FINDING* – SKILLED NEGOTIATORS MAKE LOWER CONCESSIONS AS THE DEADLINE APPROACHES.*

As pressure mounts, skilled men appear to have greater control of their concession behavior than do unskilled men. The unskilled bargainer made astounding concessions as the deadline approached. Many held firm through the session only to yield large dollar amounts at the last moment.

6. *FINDING* – A VERY HIGH UNEXPECTED INITIAL DEMAND TENDS TO LEAD TO SUCCESS RATHER THAN FAILURE OR DEADLOCK.

In this experiment both parties were told that the plaintiff was to make an initial demand of $1,075,000. A few plaintiffs chose to start at $2 million. They won handily. Unfortunately, only seven men tried this sophisticated form of "low-balling." Five won heavily, one deadlocked and one lost—but did quite well for a loser. The number of cases is not large enough to be significant but deserves further study.

Sellers are surprisingly successful when they raise an initial proposed price based upon so-called new information. This technique tends to force the buying team into the position of begging the seller to be reasonable—that is, to accept his original asking price. Hitler used the same tactic against Chamberlain and succeeded in winning almost all of Czechoslovakia instead of the smaller territory he had originally demanded.

EXPLOITATION OF POWER—RESULTS

QUESTION – Is power exploited differently by skilled and unskilled negotiators?

1. *FINDING* – UNSKILLED NEGOTIATORS IMPROVED WHEN THEY HAD MORE POWER, BUT SKILLED NEGOTIATORS DID NOT.*

This result was surprising. Figure 1 shows the large improvement made by unskilled bargainers. The average settlement of the unskilled rose from $198,000 to $429,000 when they gained power.

2. *FINDING* – THE DIFFERENCE IN PERFORMANCE BETWEEN SKILLED AND UNSKILLED NEGOTIATORS BECOMES LESS WHEN BOTH POSSESS GREATER POWER THAN THEIR RESPECTIVE OPPONENTS.

Figure 1 shows how bargaining skill becomes *less* important as more power is acquired. If plaintiff power had been increased still more, it is possible that unskilled plaintiffs might have outperformed those with skill.

3. *FINDING* – SKILLED NEGOTIATORS WITH POWER WERE BENEVOLENT TO UNSKILLED OPPONENTS.

Skilled plaintiffs with equal power scored $518,000. When they had more power they scored only $498,000. Obviously they did not exploit their new-found power. However, in those cases where they faced coached defendants who were told to be aggressive, they apparently became concerned enough to improve the settlement to $574,000. Unfortunately, the coached sample was not large enough to be meaningful.

SKILL AND SUCCESS UNDER EQUAL POWER— RESULTS

QUESTIONS – A) *Does the skill of a negotiator determine outcome under equal power?*

B) *Does the difference in the amount of skill between opponents determine outcome under equal power?*

1. FINDING – THE MORE SKILLED THE NEGOTIATOR, THE MORE HE WON. TRAIT SCORE WAS CORRELATED WITH OUTCOME.*

Under equal power, bargaining skill was a *critical* factor in determining final outcome: the best men obtained the highest settlements. Figure 1 shows that skilled plaintiffs under equal power received $518,000, while unskilled plaintiffs averaged a mere $198,000.

2. FINDING – THE LARGER THE DIFFERENCE IN THE AMOUNT OF SKILL BETWEEN OPPONENTS, THE MORE THE SKILLED MAN WON AGAINST AN ADVERSARY OF EQUAL POWER.*

Skilled men outperform unskilled men when they have *equal* power. When skilled men are fortunate enough to oppose those with far less ability, they manage to do even better.

SKILL AND SUCCESS UNDER UNEQUAL POWER—RESULTS

QUESTIONS – A) *Does the skill of a negotiator determine outcome under unequal power?*

B) *Does the difference in the amount of skill between opponents determine outcome under unequal power?*

1. FINDING – SKILLED PLAINTIFFS WITH POWER WERE ONLY

SLIGHTLY MORE SUCCESSFUL THAN UNSKILLED PLAINTIFFS
WITH POWER.

Skilled and unskilled men with power performed almost equally well. Figure 1 shows that skilled men averaged $498,-000 while unskilled men averaged $429,000. This difference is negligible.

2. *FINDING* – UNDER UNEQUAL POWER THE DIFFERENCE IN THE AMOUNT OF SKILL BETWEEN OPPONENTS WAS UNIMPORTANT EXCEPT AS FOLLOWS:

a) THE MORE INFERIOR THE LESS SKILLED NEGOTIATOR (WITH POWER), THE MORE HE EXPLOITED HIS SKILLED OPPONENT.*

b) THE MORE SUPERIOR THE SKILLED NEGOTIATOR (WITH POWER), THE MORE HE TENDED TO BE BENEVOLENT.

Two strange results occurred. In test a), unskilled men with power exploited opponents with far greater skill to a larger extent than those more on their own level. Perhaps this is what happened in Germany under Hitler when hoodlums acquired power. In test b), skilled men with superior power tended to be more benevolent to opponents who were quite inferior, but were less benevolent to those on their own skill level.

ESTIMATING RESULTS

QUESTION – *Can skilled negotiators estimate what an opponent wants better than those less skilled?*

1. *FINDING* – SKILLED AND UNSKILLED NEGOTIATORS ESTIMATE THE WANTS OF AN OPPONENT POORLY. BOTH ESTIMATED THE WANTS OF AN OPPONENT ON THE BASIS OF THEIR OWN WANTS, NOT THE OPPONENT'S.*

Even when a skilled negotiator attempts to estimate what

the other party wants, he fails because he perceives the situation in terms of his own desires. The correlation between what a negotiator himself wanted and what he *thought* the opponent wanted was very high. The fable among negotiators that a good man knows what the opponent really wants was not confirmed.

SETTLEMENT TIME — RESULTS

QUESTION – Is settlement time related to success?

1. *FINDING* – EXTREMELY QUICK SETTLEMENTS RESULT IN EXTREME OUTCOMES.*

Quick settlements resulted in very high or low outcomes rather than agreements in the middle range.

2. *FINDING* – SETTLEMENT OCCURS SHORTLY BEFORE DEADLINE.*

A significant number of settlements occurred in the last five minutes of bargaining. The establishment of time limits apparently forces agreement.

3. *FINDING* – EXTREMELY QUICK SETTLEMENTS TEND TO FAVOR SKILLED NEGOTIATORS.

Although the data is insufficient to be conclusive, skilled men won most quick settlements. Further research is necessary to determine whether negotiations of long duration are won by skilled bargainers.

DEADLOCK — RESULTS

QUESTION – How are deadlock, success, and failure related?

1. *FINDING* – PERSONS WITH EXTREMELY HIGH ASPIRATIONS FAIL LESS. THEY SUCCEED OR DEADLOCK MORE OFTEN THAN THOSE WHO WANT LESS.*

Plaintiffs who aspired to $750,000 or more rarely lost.

They achieved high settlements or deadlocked in the process. A man who wants to buy a $20,000 house in a $50,000 neighborhood may never find one. But if he buys a livable house, it will surely be a bargain. In life, a man who aspires to great heights has a better chance of success than one who does not, provided he doesn't get a "nervous breakdown" in the process.

2. *FINDING* – PERSONS WITH EXTREMELY HIGH ASPIRATIONS WHO POSSESS POWER SUCCEED PHENOMENALLY IF THEY DO NOT DEADLOCK.*

Powerful plaintiffs who aspired to $750,000 or more achieved average outcomes of $649,000. Powerful plaintiffs who aspired to less than $750,000 averaged only $370,000. However, almost half of the high aspirants deadlocked.

3. *FINDING* – OBSTINATE PERSONS DEADLOCK MORE FRE-QUENTLY THAN CONCILIATORY PERSONS, BUT FAIL LESS.*

Persons who conceded in very small amounts were either successful or they deadlocked. They rarely failed.

4. *FINDING* – WHERE ONE OR BOTH PARTIES HAVE EX-TREMELY HIGH ASPIRATIONS THE PROBABILITY OF DEADLOCK IS HIGHER THAN IF NEITHER PARTY HAS HIGH ASPIRATIONS.*

A high-aspiration negotiator is successful when he meets an opponent with low aspirations. If, however, the opponent also has high aspirations, deadlock frequently occurs. When both parties have moderate aspirations, deadlock is *not* likely to occur.

SATISFACTION WITH AGREEMENT—RESULTS

QUESTION – *Do successful and unsuccessful negotiators report equal satisfaction with a final agreement?*

1. *FINDING* – WINNERS AND LOSERS EXPRESSED EQUAL SATIS-FACTION.

Both parties reported equal satisfaction with the outcome even when one did exceedingly well and the other poorly. In real life most people appear to express satisfaction with the outcome of a negotiation even when we as outside observers consider the outcome one-sided.

PUTTING THE EXPERIMENT TO WORK

As practical men of action, each of us feels a need to put newly found knowledge to work on today's opportunities. The major findings of this experiment will provide the negotiator and his top management with some new ways to look at age-old challenges.

First, we discovered that skilled negotiators were very successful when they had high aspirations or were lucky enough to face unskilled opponents with equal power.

Second, we found that skilled negotiators were benevolent when they had power.

Third, we found that unskilled negotiators were losers except when they had power *and* high aspirations.

Fourth, we discovered that successful negotiators made high initial demands, avoided making first concessions, conceded slowly and avoided making as many large concessions as did their opponents.

Fifth, our results indicate that successful negotiators used concession in a dynamic way. They applied the above techniques to test the validity of their own assumptions and the intent of the opponent. Losers did not test reality in the same way. Both were equally poor estimators.

Sixth, all negotiators, successful or not, expressed equal satisfaction with the final agreement.

An experiment is not reality. Although the subjects fought hard, little was at issue except personal pride—money, position and public honor were not at stake. Perhaps it was the fact that they were professionals that caused them to bargain as seriously as they did. But one can never be sure that men will do their best work under game conditions. On the other hand, those who negotiated for the Starmatic Company in Chapter 1 were not as serious about a real-life situation as they should have been.

Make no mistake, this experiment is but a minor link in a growing chain of knowledge. With experimental and analytical work of the highest order conducted by social scientists and economists, each passing day provides new insight into the negotiation process.

CHAPTER 3

WHAT MAKES A GOOD NEGOTIATOR?

USE SUCH PERSONS AS AFFECT THE BUSINESS WHEREIN THEY ARE EMPLOYED; FOR THAT QUICKENETH MUCH: AND SUCH AS ARE FIT FOR THE MATTER; AS BOLD MEN FOR EXPOSTULATION, FAIR-SPOKEN MEN FOR PERSUASION, CRAFTY MEN FOR INQUIRY AND OBSERVATION, AND AB-SURD MEN FOR BUSINESS THAT DOTH NOT WELL BEAR OUT ITSELF. USE ALSO SUCH AS HAVE BEEN LUCKY, AND PREVAILED BEFORE IN THINGS WHEREIN YOU HAVE EM-PLOYED THEM: FOR THAT BREEDS CONFIDENCE, AND THEY WILL STRIVE TO MAINTAIN THEIR PRESCRIPTION.

Sir Francis Bacon

THE FAULT, DEAR BRUTUS, IS NOT IN OUR STARS, BUT IN OURSELVES. . . .

Shakespeare

What are the traits of an effective negotiator? How do the opinions of buyers, salesmen, engineers, contract managers and purchasing executives differ in this regard? Do attorneys, accountants, retail buyers and real-estate salesmen see a negotiator in the same light?

To get answers, three opinion polls were conducted among

these groups. In addition, the literature of diplomacy, business and collective bargaining was probed for a deeper insight into the personality makeup of successful men in general. As a result of these studies we are now able to do two things that could not be done before: 1) *measure* bargaining skill objectively, and 2) understand how the attitudes of these various professional groups differ with respect to the qualities necessary for a first-rate negotiator.

Newsweek recently described Arthur Goldberg as follows: "1) Very likable, 2) very knowledgeable, 3) catches on very quickly, 4) penetrates the real issues, 5) is resourceful and 6) is persuasive."[2] It would be nice if all of us were so blessed. Yet, the list leaves questions unanswered. Is knowledge as important as catching on quickly, or three times as important? Is persuasiveness less valuable than resourcefulness? Few men possess all these traits in equal abundance. Which, if any, can be compromised? Could a man be effective if he were not knowledgeable but possessed other attributes?

To further complicate the matter, the Goldberg list might well have included such qualities as patience, self-control, confidence and planning ability, for these are traits men rightly value. For centuries diplomats and businessmen have wrestled with the question of ideal traits in their search for the perfect ambassador or executive. It is not surprising that the characteristics of both are almost identical, for they spend much of their time negotiating.

HOW BUSINESSMEN LOOK AT EXECUTIVE TRAITS

Frederick W. Taylor, the father of scientific management, discovered an unusual solution to the problem of finding an *ideal* executive. He suggested that an employee be supervised by eight men rather than one. In his theory, each functional

supervisor would apply those qualities and special skills necessary to do the job. Managers laughed at the idea in 1900 and
are still laughing today, but not quite as heartily. The idea
appears less absurd in this modern age of extreme specializa-
tion. One has only to look at procedure manuals to note that
personnel, purchasing and other staff specialists exert direct
influence on the behavior of men engaged in line activities.
Today's worker takes orders from not eight but perhaps eight-
een staff specialists.

While there continues to be controversy among businessmen, a few executive traits emerge as most essential. Executives should be achievement-oriented, decisive, intelligent,
well organized, imaginative, confident, sensitive and tolerant
of uncertainty. Needless to say, on this basis few of us are
likely to be overqualified.

AMBASSADORS LOOK AT DIPLOMATIC TRAITS

The relationship between diplomacy and negotiation is
so close that Webster's defines diplomacy as "the practice of
conducting negotiations between nations." Diplomatic literature is rich in perceptive observation and examples. Sir Harold
Nicolson, a respected English diplomat, summarized the
modern viewpoint by listing seven special qualities necessary
to a skillful emissary: truthfulness, moral accuracy, calmness,
tolerance, patience, dignity and loyalty. In addition, he *assumes*
that the diplomat will also possess a high degree of intelligence,
knowledge, discernment, prudence, charm and courage. Nicolson's view does not differ much from the ideas expressed centuries earlier by French and Italian diplomats.[3]

Until recently there has been little serious trait research
done. Perhaps due in part to the "Ugly American" image
abroad, government grants have been provided to focus disciplined attention on diplomatic qualities. In California a

group of social scientists have used computers to conduct studies relating bargaining behavior to personality. They have developed a personality-attitude test that measures such traits as aggressiveness, risk-avoidance, self-control and suspiciousness. There is preliminary evidence that such measures are related to outcome.[4] For example, bargaining pairs composed of persons scoring high in conciliation and risk-avoidance achieved higher total payments for both parties than pairs composed of persons low in these traits. Further research is likely to provide greater insight and thereby improve our ability to select good diplomats.

THE FIRST SURVEY—SENIOR PURCHASING EXECUTIVES

An experiment that attempts to find a relationship between ability and outcome is likely to be meaningless unless skill can be measured objectively. It was not enough to match men on the basis that they were good or bad or in-between. In order to apply a numerical measure to ability, three answers were necessary:

1. Which traits are important?
2. How does each trait *rank* in importance?
3. How much more important is one trait than another (weight)?

A decision was made to obtain answers by taking a survey of high-level purchasing executives—that is, men who have themselves engaged in large transactions and commanded subordinates as well.

Prior to the survey, traits were divided into six clusters, each containing seven or eight attributes. Included among the *Task-Performance* traits were stamina, planning, knowledge, problem-solving and goal-striving. The *Aggression* group in-cluded the ability to perceive and exploit power, persistence, courage, leadership, competitiveness and risk-taking behavior. *Socializing* qualities were represented by sense of humor, personal attractiveness, interpersonal integrity and cooperative-ness. The *Communication* cluster consisted of skills associated with verbal and nonverbal expression: listening, debate and role-playing ability. *Self-Worth* attributes included the ability to win the confidence of one's opponent as well as one's su-perior, personal dignity, self-control and self-esteem. In the *Thought-Process* cluster were judgment, insight, decisiveness and ability to think clearly under pressure. A total of 45 traits were represented in the six categories.

Twenty-six senior executives were asked to rank traits within clusters from *most* to *least* essential. In addition, they chose four traits among the 45 as most important. From the response it was possible to answer the question of trait rank and weight. For instance, planning skill was found to be thir-teen times as important as stamina and almost twice as im-portant as individual initiative or problem-solving ability. The ability to express thoughts verbally was considered almost twice as valuable as debating ability. Insight was ten times as beneficial as education and considerably more essential than experience. Data from the first survey is shown in Table 2.

NEGOTIATOR TRAIT RANK AND WEIGHTS
(HIGHEST LEVEL PURCHASING EXECUTIVES). Table 2

TASK-PERFORMANCE CLUSTER		
Rank	*Weight*	
1	15.0	Planning
2	8.3	Problem-solving
3	7.8	Goal-striving
4	7.7	Initiative
5	6.4	Product knowledge
6	3.4	Reliability
7	1.2	Stamina

AGGRESSION CLUSTER

Rank	Weight	
1	13.0	Power exploitation
2	9.3	Competitiveness
3	8.9	Team leadership
4	5.8	Persistence
5	5.0	Risk-taking
6	3.5	Courage
7	1.6	Defensiveness

SOCIALIZING CLUSTER

Rank	Weight	
1	13.1	Personal integrity
2	11.0	Open-minded
3	10.3	Tact
4	7.8	Patience
5	7.7	Personal attractiveness
6	4.8	Appearance
7	4.1	Compromising
8	1.5	Trust

COMMUNICATION CLUSTER

Rank	Weight	
1	11.9	Verbal clarity
2	9.3	Listening
3	9.3	Coordinating skill
4	8.2	Warm rapport
5	6.9	Debating
6	5.2	Role-playing
7	1.5	Nonverbal

SELF-WORTH CLUSTER

Rank	Weight	
1	11.9	Gain opponent's respect
2	10.0	Self-esteem
3	9.4	Self-control
4	8.8	Ethical standard
5	6.2	Personal dignity
6	5.0	Gain boss's respect
7	3.9	Risk being disliked
8	1.7	Organizational rank

		THOUGHT-PROCESS CLUSTER
Rank	*Weight*	
1	12.2	Clear thinking under stress
2	12.2	General practical intelligence
3	10.0	Insight
4	8.9	Analytical ability
5	7.0	Decisiveness
6	6.5	Negotiating experience
7	5.4	Broad perspective
8	1.0	Education

Purchasing executives were in general agreement that a good negotiator must possess, *above all else,* a high degree of planning ability. They were *least* concerned with his education, stamina and nonverbal-communication skills. As a result of this survey we were, for the first time, in a position to understand the relative importance of various traits. In addition, it was possible to use the data to measure negotiating skill in a more objective fashion.

HOW OTHER PROFESSIONS SEE NEGOTIATION

The next opinion polls were designed to discover how people in different professions look at bargaining traits. The basic question was, "How do the attitudes of salesmen, engineers, buyers and contract-management people differ?" What about lawyers, accountants and retail buyers in the clothing industry?

Four hundred and eighty-three professional negotiators responded. The results were analyzed statistically and are shown in appendixes I and II at the back of the book. You will not be surprised to learn that there were significant differences between groups.

DIFFERENCES AMONG INDUSTRIAL NEGOTIATORS

Program managers, design engineers and supplier representatives emerged as entrepreneural types while the other industrial groups did not. Engineering program managers were particularly individualistic. They placed greater emphasis on objectives, ability to exploit power, willingness to take risks and the need for discretion. They placed less stress on the importance of business integrity and little weight on the ability to create close personal rapport with an opponent. Program managers were opportunity-oriented.

The design engineer's profile is almost as individualistic as the program manager's. Design engineers stressed product knowledge, self-control, discretion and perspective. They severely downgraded insight, close personal rapport and risk-taking. They emerged as men considerably more attuned to facts and objectives than to the social aspects of negotiation. Furthermore, those who are familiar with the high-safety factors often built into engineering specifications will not be surprised to learn that design engineers do not like to take risks at the bargaining table either.

Supplier salesmen emerged as tough competitors. They placed special value on product knowledge, persistence, intelligence and business ethics but downgraded problem-solving skills, debating ability and decisiveness. Supplier representatives appear to be men who make a persistent effort to gain objectives. They perceive negotiation as a contest of knowledge and objectives in contrast to the buyers who place greater emphasis on the problem-solving and decisiveness aspects.

A fundamental difference in attitude exists between engineering program managers and purchasing executives along two dimensions. Program managers show a strong willingness to risk being disliked while purchasing executives do not. In addition, the latter express greater concern for ethics. It is not surprising that value conflicts arise between these functions.

A similar but less serious division exists between contract managers and program managers. Contract administrators value caution, ethics and persistence while program managers place less emphasis on these virtues and more on self-esteem and the willingness to risk being disliked. Contract managers appear to be more bureaucratic in temperament than the men for whom they negotiate.

DIFFERENCES AMONG COMMERCIAL NEGOTIATORS

Commercial negotiators—that is, attorneys, accountants, real-estate salesmen and retail-clothing buyers—viewed negotiation in much the same way as those engaged in the industrial field, with several notable exceptions. As a group, those in commercial activities placed greater emphasis on analytical ability, self-esteem and patience. The differences between various professions is tabulated in appendix II and summarized below.

Attorneys and accountants see negotiation as a problem-solving affair rather than as a quest for reaching objectives. No other professions surveyed were so emphatic on these points. It should be noted that the real-estate and retail-buying professions were outstandingly objective-oriented.

Real-estate people value initiative and willingness to take risks more than most groups, but attach least significance to planning. They and retail clothing buyers emerged as the individualists of the commercial group.

As the survey is expanded, two points become clear: 1) the difference in opinion between various professions is significant, and 2) when members of different professions assist one another at the bargaining table they are likely to view negotiation traits in diverse ways. A good team leader will resolve these differences early and thereby avert conflict at the bargaining table.

ASK A WOMAN

When in doubt, ask a woman. Since men spend half their lives negotiating with women, I decided to find out what they thought. The results will not surprise those of us long married. They expect us to plan well, know much about the subject under discussion, take the initiative, try hard to reach our goals and show good judgment in the process. They do not lack for aspirations in what they wish for us.

Although most men ranked integrity among the four most important traits, women assigned it a lesser place. Perhaps some sociologist will ask them why—not I.

CONCLUSION

Those who know most about negotiation, the professionals, have spoken. They collectively believe that the following seven traits are most important:

- Planning skill
- Ability to think clearly under stress
- General practical intelligence
- Verbal ability
- Product knowledge
- Personal integrity
- Ability to perceive and exploit power

From my experience and reading I would not quarrel with these findings except to add a few that I consider essential. A negotiator must think well of himself. This feeling of self-worth should come from a history of getting things done satisfactorily and faith in one's ability to understand and re-solve the fundamental values being negotiated.

The ideal negotiator should have a high tolerance for ambiguity and uncertainty as well as the open-mindedness to test his own assumptions and the opponent's intentions. This requires courage. Finally, in every good negotiator there must be an inner desire to achieve, to aspire, to take that sensible but extra measure of risk that represents a commitment to one's strivings. As Shakespeare said, "And pay the debt I never promised"— to ourselves and those we represent.

The Heart
of the
Bargaining
Process

INTRODUCTION TO PART II.   Imagine for a moment that you are a doctor looking at this living, breathing thing called negotiation. You want to understand what makes it work and why. Where do you start?

On the surface, clearly visible, like external parts of the body, are the two negotiators and their conflicting demands. Also evident are techniques such as concession and threat as well as a copious display of oratorical fireworks. Less apparent are the internal organs. In every complex living thing there lurks beneath the easily visible a net of interlinking systems that preserve, maintain and enhance its being. So it is with negotiation. To understand this subject we must go beneath the surface to those elements that are common to all bargaining transactions.

In Part II we will look at the heart of the bargaining process. Our eyepiece will be focused on aspiration level, goal-setting, power, persuasion and other aspects of the anatomy of negotiation. Only when these central elements of the process are better understood will it be possible for us to speak intelligently about strategy and tactics.

CHAPTER 4

WHAT'S
YOUR ASPIRATION
LEVEL?

THAT LOW MAN SEEKS A LITTLE THING TO DO,
    SEES IT AND DOES IT:
THIS HIGH MAN, WITH A GREAT THING TO PURSUE,
    DIES ERE HE KNOWS IT.

THAT LOW MAN GOES ON ADDING ONE TO ONE,
    HIS HUNDREDS SOON HIT;
THIS HIGH MAN, AIMING AT A MILLION,
    MISSES A UNIT.

                     Robert Browning

    I WORKED FOR A MENIAL'S HIRE,
    ONLY TO LEARN, DISMAYED,
    THAT ANY WAGE I HAD ASKED OF LIFE,
    LIFE WOULD HAVE PAID.

                 Jessie B. Rittenhouse

About forty years ago some of the finest minds of the twentieth century began to wonder why some people were *under-achievers* at school and at work. Their attention soon became focused on the question of aspiration level and success. Recently two professors tried an experiment.[5] They built a barricade between bargainers so that neither could see or hear the other. Demands and offers were passed under the table. Instructions to both were identical, with one exception: one was told he was expected to achieve a $7.50 settlement and the other $2.50. The experiment was designed to favor neither party—that is, both had an *equal* chance to get $5.00. What happened? *Men who expected $7.50 got $7.50 while those told to expect $2.50 got $2.50.*

The conditions in the experiment described in Chapter 2 were different. Where the professors' subjects were students, ours were professionals; where they limited communication between negotiators, we created face-to-face encounter; where they induced an artificial level of aspiration, we let each man decide for himself. What good negotiators know will happen happened: subjects with high aspirations got high settlements; those who wanted little got little.

Interestingly, those who were successful and those who were not expressed equal satisfaction with the outcome. I cannot recall the last time a negotiator returned from a conference and reported dissatisfaction with an agreement. When people want and expect less, they are satisfied with less. John Masefield, the English poet, may have had this in mind when he said, "Success is the brand on the brow of the man who aimed too low."

In life, as in negotiation, it appears that those with high aspirations reach higher goals. The question we must ask is, "Do men bring lifelong aspiration patterns into the conference room?" I believe they do. There is a growing body of evidence that supports this contention.

The time has come to consider aspiration level in its relationship to goal-setting, risk-taking, self-esteem, persistence and success. Of all the journeys into negotiation, this is perhaps the finest trip of all.

GOAL-SETTING BEHAVIOR

People set goals for themselves even when they are un-aware they are doing so. The person deciding between an Oldsmobile and a Cadillac is saying something about his status goals. The person deciding between dropping out of high school or continuing through college is assigning himself a place in society. The executive willing to tolerate a mediocre staff is indicating his own standard. Our role is to learn how people set goals and to apply this knowledge to negotiation.

An individual's level of aspiration represents his *intended* performance goal. It is a reflection of how much he wants—that is, a standard he sets for himself. *It is not a wish but a firm intention to perform that involves his self-image.* Failure to perform results in loss of self-respect. Given such a harsh definition of "aspiration level," we will direct our attention to how goals are established.

We should imagine an athlete who has just run the 100-yard dash in ten seconds. If the runner is competitive he is likely to try for 9.9 seconds in his next race. If the next race is run in ten seconds he will experience disappointment. On the other hand the runner will be elated if he lowers his record. Thus we see four steps in goal-setting: 1) starting per-formance (ten seconds), 2) establishing a level of aspiration (9.9 seconds), 3) subsequent performance (9.9 seconds) and 4) feelings of success.

Americans are racing through life trying to maintain or exceed present levels of achievement. We set targets for occupa-tion, income, status and power. The world provides a quick feedback, thereby causing us to continuously reassess our aspiration levels and set new goals.

A *Fortune* study asked people about their lifetime-income goals. Men earning $5,000 a year reported they would be happy with slightly more than $5,000. Men earning $20,000 a year wanted slightly more than $20,000. Each income level revealed that their level of aspiration was directly related to *present* earnings. The poor did not aspire to income levels of the middle classes. They assigned themselves to the lower classes on the basis of past performance. *Level of aspiration is a yardstick by which we measure ourselves.*

GROUP MEMBERSHIP AND ASPIRATION

Although aspiration level is an *individual matter,* one can hardly think about it without recognizing that objectives are not established in a social vacuum. Group membership plays an important role in providing the frame of reference by which people decide the appropriateness of their targets.

A man may decide *how much he wants* in three ways: 1) on the basis of his own past performance, 2) on the basis of the performance of other members in his direct group and 3) on the basis of the performance of those in reference groups to which he would like to belong.

For example, an executive may set an income target on the basis of his present salary, $25,000 per year, or that of other executives in aerospace, $28,000, or that of executives doing the same work in rapidly growing conglomerates, $35,000 plus stock options. In any case, once a reference target is chosen, it becomes a yardstick by which self-esteem is measured.

Corporations set goals in the same way. That is why it is so important for a company to have a self-image. An 8 percent return on an investment may be fine if a company is comparing itself to a group of old-line competitors. On the other hand, the 8 percent return can look pretty bad when measured against an aggressive organization such as Republic Corporation. *Executives must not only ask where they stand,* but *compared with whom.*

In negotiation it is only rarely possible to compare one's performance with that of others. Comparisons are, of course, possible where precedent decisions have been made or other guidelines exist. A negotiator normally has some data to guide him, but the *range of uncertainty* is so large and subject to so much interpretation on fairly complex deals that outside reference points are not as useful. In fact they may actually be dangerous, for they may lull the negotiator into a false sense of security and cause him to accept inappropriate agreements.

Group membership plays a role in establishing negotiation targets because it is invariably a decision group that participates in the goal-setting process. Each member of the decision group has a different aspiration level. *Team objectives are themselves a product of negotiation between decision-group members.* It is essential to recognize that all organization goals, negotiation and otherwise, are determined by a group-bargaining process.

SUCCESS AND FAILURE

Each demand and concession contributes to an opponent's feelings about success or failure. It is therefore worthwhile to know more about the mechanism by which success is experienced. Three points should be understood.

First, success is relative. It depends upon what is wanted. I consider myself pretty successful if I can wake up and go to work. My neighbor considers himself a failure unless he runs two miles before breakfast. In the experiment, some men insisted that they would accept nothing less than $700,000 while others were quite content with $200,000. As the psychologist Alfred Adler said, "What an individual feels as success is unique with him."

Second, people typically raise aspirations after success and reduce them after failure. If they enjoy a great success, they tend to set much higher goals than if success is moderate. When failure is moderate, there is a tendency for people to reduce aspirations slightly. A massive failure is normally followed, however, by a sharp drop in aspiration level.

Third, a person does not experience success or failure every time he does something. He gets little satisfaction from doing a simple task and feels no sense of defeat if the job is too far above his capability. Only if a task lies close to the upper limit of his ability does a man become involved enough to feel good or bad about performance. It follows that behind every experience of suc´ ss or failure lies conflict. On the one hand a person tends to set lower targets because he fears failure; on the other he tends to set higher targets because he desires success.[6]

It is wise to consider every maneuver and technique in terms of its effect on the opponent's feelings about success and failure. A moderate offer on the negotiator's part may be considered a massive success by an opponent who has low aspirations and may encourage him to revise his goals upward to unrealistic limits. Everything that is done during negotiation should be designed to change the opponent's level of aspiration in the desired direction through the success-failure mechanism. More will be said in Chapter 14 about how techniques like concession can be designed to affect the opponent's aspiration level and concept of success.

THE ACHIEVEMENT MOTIVE AND SUCCESS

Some years ago the fiery leader of the Soviet Union, Nikita Khrushchev, made a dramatic visit to the United States. Everywhere he went he made trouble. When invited to a dinner by the Mayor of Los Angeles, Khrushchev treated his hosts to a speech on how the Soviet Union was going to "bury" the United States. After visiting a film studio he came away announcing disgust at our vulgar taste in producing something as silly as

"Can Can." However, Khrushchev made one speech in which he was profoundly correct, although the point made was not what he had intended.

The Soviet leader, when asked to give a short address to luncheon guests of the movie tycoon Spyros Skouras, decided that he would contrast a Soviet industrial commissar in his group with the host. The Russian asked his commissar to stand up in front of television cameras and then proceeded to tell the American people that this immensely powerful representative of Soviet industrial might was more productive than Skouras but owned nothing but the pants he stood in. For once Khrushchev was right, but it took a profound study by a distinguished American psychologist to prove his point.

David C. McClelland in his fine book, *The Achieving Society,* points out that persons with strong achievement drives demand more of themselves in performing challenging tasks.[7] They work harder, do a better job and value accomplishment more than reward. High-need-for-achievement individuals want rapid feedback from their work. They are interested in money as a symbol of successful accomplishment and not as an end in itself. Furthermore, McClelland found that successful executives everywhere, communist, socialist or capitalist, were high in need for achievement. In that sense Khrushchev implied that Spyros Skouras, had he been a Russian, would have been a mighty commissar with one pair of pants. As we shall soon see, success, need for achievement, expectations and aspiration level are intimately related.

RISK-TAKING AND EXPECTATION

How do you find your wife in the department store when you lose her? Thomas C. Schelling believes that to find her you *do not* go to where you think she is. Instead, you ask yourself where you expect her to go based on her expectations about

where you will go. Schelling is convinced that real world negotiations are settled when expectations of both parties converge
as they do in his department-store illustration.[8] Perhaps we
should have settled the Vietnam war in 1965 by letting President Johnson find Ho Chi Minh in Macy's department store
during the Christmas rush. Be that as it may, there is little
question that expectations play a crucial role in bargaining,
particularly in the area of risk-taking and aspiration level.

Expectations are associated with the achievement motive.
People with a high need for achievement behave as though they
expect success. John W. Atkinson, a colleague of McClelland,
posed this question: "I know that people with a high need for
achievement tend to be successful but I want to know how they
actually behave in ways that turn out well?" He developed a
theory that involved expectation, risk, achievement motive and
incentives.[9]

Atkinson reasoned that men are torn between the rewards
that come from success and the dangers that come from failure.
They are driven by a desire for success and a fear of failure.
People choose goals that are likely to provide the most personal
satisfaction considering 1) need for achievement, 2) reward,
3) risk of failure and 4) expectations of success. People cannot
make this computation consciously. Instead, they reason it out
as best they can based on their past history of success and
failure in similar situations.

The *Atkinson Aspiration Model*, shown in Figure 2, says
that individuals set their aspiration level by evaluating the
pleasure of success against the displeasure of failure. They
strive to reach goals that maximize the total attractiveness of
the task. However, the first thing that strikes us about the
diagram is that persons with a strong desire for success do not
look at risk in the same way as those who stress the avoidance
of failure. The success type prefers risks in the 50–50 range
while the failure-type prefers short or long odds. Success-
oriented people maximize task attractiveness by setting their

level of aspiration where they can attribute success to their own abilities. People with a high fear of failure avoid reasonable challenges because it threatens their self-image. If they set low goals, they cannot fail. If they set goals so high that the probability of success is slight, they can feel comforted by the fact that failure was inevitable anyway. In either case their goal-setting behavior preserves rather than threatens self-esteem.

Experiments have confirmed much of this theory. Investigators found that achievement types are optimistic and tend to overestimate the likelihood of success while fear-of-failure types do not. Success-oriented people, in contrast to those who fear failure, *do not* like pure gambling, for they get little satisfaction from winning when their own skill is not involved.

Related studies confirm that individuals tend to estimate probability of success in terms of hopes as well as facts. When they want something very badly, they overestimate their chances of getting it. When people were asked, "What score would you like to get next time?" they were not as *realistic*

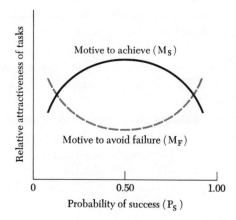

Figure 2. ATKINSON ASPIRATION MODEL

in setting goals as those who were asked, "What score do you expect to get next time?" In one case self-image was involved; in the other it was not.

On the basis of Atkinson's research we are in a better position to see how people with high achievement needs behave in ways that turn out well. Achievement-oriented individuals approach tasks in a confident manner. Having been successful in the past, they are enthusiastic about new challenges involving personal skill. They are willing to stake their self-image on risks in the 50–50 range. The fear-of-failure person is pessimistic; having been somewhat of a loser all along, he is afraid to stake his self-image on the next contest. He therefore prefers risks where the probability of success is high or low rather than in the middle range.

In negotiation, success-oriented people will tend to set targets higher and be more optimistic of their chances for success. The others will find ways to play it safe.

PERSISTENCE AND ASPIRATION

A negotiator enters the conference room with a level of aspiration and adjusts his goals in response to encouragement or frustration. Most men raise aspirations when they succeed and lower their sights when they fail. The degree to which they follow this typical pattern differs because some men are more persistent than others.

Experiments indicate that success-oriented men are not always persistent. When a task is easy they quickly lose interest. On the other hand, achievement-oriented persons were found to be more persistent when a task was thought to be easy but proved frustrating. They enjoyed the unexpected challenge and responded to overcome it.

Fear-of-failure persons tend to persist longer when the

odds against success are very long or very short. They are less persistent in the middle range of success probability.

In our experiment, skilled men with power did not exploit unskilled opponents. The explanation may lie in the Atkinson aspiration theory, which predicts that success-oriented negotiators would lose interest as success became assured. A review of the concession data indicated that low-power defendants were *conciliatory*, thereby causing the powerful skilled plaintiffs to lose interest even faster.

The same thing happens in sports occasionally when a top team is defeated by a third-rate competitor. John Wooden, basketball coach of the college-champion UCLA Bruins, attributed his team's two defeats in 100 games to the letdown associated with a string of easy victories prior to the losses.

Atkinson's experimental studies indicate that persistence, expectation and risk-taking are related. For those who manage men who negotiate, the findings should give rise to thought. Skilled men lose interest in tasks that offer little chance of success. They give up more quickly than their less gifted counterparts. Perhaps that is why Sir Francis Bacon cautioned the prince to use "absurd men for business that doth not well bear out itself." Be that as it may, in our experiment highly skilled men who faced more powerful opponents were pessimistic, lowered their aspirations and did not do well.

REALISM, ASPIRATION AND MENTAL HEALTH

It's good to have high aspirations, but it's not good if they are so high as to be unrealistic. There are many people in mental hospitals whose aspirations outstripped their capabilities. The reality of daily living is a stern taskmaster that provides rapid feedback to those whose goals are unrealistic.

A person's mental health is related to his self-esteem. The

tendency to raise aspiration levels as high as possible is closely related to self-esteem. An individual's level of aspiration is determined by his ability and his history of success and failure.

Mentally healthy people tend to accept themselves in a favorable light. They have a sense of self-identity, know how to test reality and how meet their needs. They set goals that are consistent with their capabilities and the demands of the outside world.

There is a growing body of evidence that mental health is related to realistic goal-setting. In 1963 a researcher classified three groups of subjects as normal, neurotic or psychotic.[10] The subjects then performed an aspiration-level task that involved shooting a pinball down a track containing a series of holes into which the ball could fall. Each hole represented a different score value. The holes were spaced so that subjects could decide for themselves whether to try for high scores with low probabilities of success or low scores with high probabilities. In a second version of the test the element of frustration was introduced by inserting magnets into the setup. These magnets deflected the balls and made it difficult to predict outcome.

The investigator discovered that realistic goals were chosen by people who were better adjusted. Maladjusted people were attracted to targets that offered little chance of success even when they *knew beyond a doubt* that the odds were very poor. Neurotics chose targets that were less realistic than those of normal persons and more realistic than those of psychotics.

All groups reacted to frustration by showing an increased tendency toward unrealistic behavior. However, it was the neurotics who were most affected. The results of this experiment were consistent with others, which indicate that people low in self-esteem perform a larger number of *unbalanced* acts under pressure than persons who think well of themselves.

It appears that stable people react to success and failure experiences in a typical fashion—that is, they raise or lower goals accordingly. Those who are not stable behave unrealistically; they sometimes raise aspirations in response to serious failure or lower their goals in response to success. In any case the mental maturity of a negotiator is directly relevant to his ability to set realistic goals.

PERSONALITY AND ASPIRATION — AN OVERVIEW

In the light of recent experimental findings we may draw some conclusions about the relationship of personality to aspiration level. The achievement-oriented person is attracted to tasks that involve skill. Unlike the gambler, he prefers to take mid-range risks and tends to be realistic. He likes to do a job well for its own sake, and he is a persistent striver who believes that hard work pays off. This type of person tends to approach ambiguous situations with confidence of success, enthusiasm and optimism.

Achievement-oriented persons take a long-term view of life. They plan and direct their energies to projects that take time to complete. They are problem-solvers and obstacle-removers, patient, determined and competitive. When they have a job to do and need help, they choose experts. On the job they tend to talk about business rather than other matters. They have a lesser need for closure and black-and-white solutions than those who are not achievement-oriented.

The achievement-oriented person expects success and therefore sets his aspiration level high. He succeeds because he is realistic, persistent and receptive to feedback.

CONCLUSION

Negotiation is one of the last frontiers of old-fashioned entrepreneurship in American business today. It is best carried out by men with a high need for achievement—that is, by men who are entrepreneurs. These are the aggressive men who get things done in our society: the reasonable risk-takers who view the challenge of negotiation more as an opportunity than a problem.

We want negotiators who will set their sights high and commit themselves to achieving their objectives. Yet we must recognize that men, even those with strong achievement needs, will not knowingly design the club with which to beat themselves to death. For that reason management must take a more courageous role in negotiating a realistic aspiration level with its own negotiators. Too often management "cops out" by telling its representatives to do the best they can. That's not good enough.

It was Shakespeare who said,

> "—OUR DOUBTS ARE TRAITORS,
> AND MAKE US LOSE THE GOOD WE OFT MIGHT WIN
> BY FEARING TO ATTEMPT."

Both management and those who negotiate must learn to test these doubts by asking each other, *"What's your aspiration level, and why?"* They will probably find that their aspirations in negotiation as in life are not as high as they should be.

CHAPTER 5

YOU
HAVE MORE POWER THAN
YOU THINK

POWER CONCEDES NOTHING WITHOUT A DEMAND. IT NEVER
DID, AND IT NEVER WILL. FIND OUT JUST WHAT PEOPLE
WILL SUBMIT TO, AND YOU HAVE FOUND OUT THE EXACT
AMOUNT OF INJUSTICE AND WRONG WHICH WILL BE IM-
POSED UPON THEM; AND THESE WILL CONTINUE TILL THEY
HAVE RESISTED WITH EITHER WORDS OR BLOWS, OR WITH
BOTH. THE LIMITS OF TYRANTS ARE PRESCRIBED BY THE
ENDURANCE OF THOSE WHOM THEY SUPPRESS.

Frederick Douglass

On August 23, 1968, President Ludvik Svoboda of Czechoslovakia told Communist Party boss Leonid I. Brezhnev in his
Kremlin office, "If I kill myself, my blood will be on your
hands and no one in the world will believe you did not murder
me." Svoboda threatened suicide unless the Russians freed the
liberal leaders whom they had seized three days earlier. The
threat was successful. According to a report released by the
Los Angeles Times on September 23, 1968, the Russians
promptly released the Czech leaders and permitted them to
participate in ensuing negotiations. Had it not been for the

courage of the seventy-three-year-old Svoboda, these men might have perished in a Moscow jail. Considering the bravery of these people against an occupying power, one cannot help wondering whether they might have held Hitler at bay thirty years earlier. Svoboda and the Czechoslovaks do not perceive power as other subjugated people do.

Power relationships exist everywhere. The form may be black, green, military or political. In this chapter we will find out what power is and why some people are intimidated by it while others are not.

Americans generally assume that the powerful party in a negotiation will exert the greatest influence. But we are beginning to wonder if this common-sense notion is true. At many universities students have captured administrative offices; in France a strike that engulfed the nation and Charles DeGaulle began with a routine demonstration at the Sorbonne; Senator McCarthy, campaigning without funds in New Hampshire, captured the imagination of Americans and helped to unseat an incumbent President; in Vietnam a fourth-rate power has successfully repulsed the United States. Power, like beauty, is to a large degree a state of mind.

THE BASIC PRINCIPLES OF POWER

One step in preparing for negotiation is to evaluate the power balance between opponents. Such an analysis is not possible unless the principles of power are understood. For practical purposes power may be defined as *the ability of a negotiator to influence the behavior of an opponent*. The eight principles listed below are applicable to most transactions.

First, power is always relative. Rarely if ever does a buyer or seller enjoy *complete* power.

Second, power may be real or apparent. The fact that a position is supported by logic, justice or force does not guarantee success. A seller may be in a preferred position, but if neither he nor the buyer perceives the advantage, he has none. Conversely, the seller may be in a weak position due to lack of business, but if the buyer does not perceive this, the buyer's power is not enhanced.

Third, power may be exerted without action. If an opponent *believes* that action can and will be taken against him, it may be unnecessary to act.

Fourth, power is always limited. Its range depends upon the situation, government regulations, ethical standards and present or future competition.

Fifth, power exists to the extent that it is accepted. A buyer who *insists* that he will not be exploited by a monopolistic seller is less likely to be victimized. Some people are simply less willing to be dominated than others and would rather do without than be exploited.

Sixth, the ends of power cannot be separated from the means. One cannot hope to develop a loyal customer by using exploitive tactics. Several years ago we did business with a ruthless supplier because it was to our best interest to do so. The supplier, an aggressive conglomerate, was aware of its bargaining position and took the occasion to be uncompromising and disrespectful to our people. It was a short-lived victory, for it is now distrusted by industry and government buyers alike.

Seventh, the exercise of power always entails cost and risk.

Eighth, power relationships change over time. The balance of power moves as the balance of benefits and contributions from the parties change.

These principles are applicable over a wide range of exchange situations. The following story illustrates many of the principles in a bargaining situation that would challenge even Arthur Goldberg.

THE ESKIMO AND THE TRADER

Peter Freuchen in *Book of the Eskimos* describes how the Eskimo negotiates. In the frozen Arctic a single trading post may service trappers hundreds of miles away. For most of the year families trap in the North Country. They return twice annually for replenishment of necessities. If ever one sought to find a true monopolist, the trader would be an ideal model.

When a trapper returns from the wilderness he carefully parks his sled in a place where townspeople can see the size of the tarp-covered load and some of its quality furs. After friendly and extensive solicitations concerning the good health of the storekeeper, the Eskimo explains how poor his catch is and how ashamed he is to offer such shoddy pelts in exchange for handsome store goods.

Although no verbal offer is made, the Eskimo walks slowly through the store pointing to items that he feels "unworthy of." Next day he repeats this process in the presence of his poor but dignified family. As the children gape at the candy jar the Eskimo again bemoans his lack of skill as a trapper, all the while continuing to congratulate the trader on the quality and diversity of his goods and pointing out that the wise trader deserves the prosperity he enjoys.

On the next day, with the trader and townspeople present, the tarp is removed. The parties then get down to business, with the Eskimo again pointing out items that he is "too humble to be worthy of" while a wordless tally is kept by both. As the bargaining proceeds the participants become more open with each other, revealing their true needs and values. After patient discussion the parties strike an agreement, deliberately leaving some matters open for future adjustment.

On his last day in town the Eskimo drops by the store to say good-bye and sadly acknowledges that he has forgotten to include some staples such as matches and candies. The trader promptly provides these items without charge. As the family is about to leave civilization once more, the trapper discovers a few superb pelts that were overlooked previously. These he provides to the trader as a departing gift.

The Eskimo knew that there are many bases of power other than competition or financial leverage.

SOURCES OF POWER

There are nine sources of strength that contribute to the overall balance of power between opponents. These are:

1. *BALANCE OF REWARDS.* Rewards may be of a tangible or intangible nature. Money, property, rights, and privileges are of a tangible nature. Financial rewards need not be expressed in profit alone but may come about as a result of goals associated with cash flow, liquidity, borrowing power, partial coverage of fixed costs, maintenance of specialized productive resources or return-on-investment targets. Rewards may also be long run—that is, a result of expanded markets, products or channels of distribution.

Intangible rewards may provide an equally important base of power. Among these are benefits that fill needs for safety, love, worth and self-realization. A sales manager's personal need to prove himself may weigh more heavily in the reward structure than the profit to be gained from the sale.

Although reward is a critical element in the balance of power, it is usually analyzed superficially. Rarely is a thorough worth-analysis made to discover the hidden factors in an opponent's reward structure. It's not easy to do a first-rate reward-analysis, but it is worthwhile to try.

2. *BALANCE OF PUNISHMENT OR NONREWARD.* One of the first lessons we learned as children is that parents can punish as well as reward. A seller can punish a buyer by circumventing his authority or by harassing him with minor

changes. A buyer can punish a seller by threatening to remove him from a bidder's list or by rejecting a product for minor quality flaws irrelevant to its end use. Deadlock is an interesting form of punishment that leaves both parties in an unpleasant state of uncertainty.

In most business transactions the parties are confronted with the possibility of losing something desirable rather than with direct punishment. A seller faced with the possibility of losing an order or a buyer denied the productive services of a valued supplier are under pressure to agree. I have attended negotiations where the central issue was not price, specification or delivery but whether we could cajole, inspire or otherwise induce the supplier to commit himself to take on the job. When times are good, reputable sellers can pick and choose their customers and often make their decision on criteria other than profit. In such a case the buyer's ability to *nonreward* the seller is minimal.

Punishment and nonreward may be tangible or intangible. When collective bargaining fails and a strike takes place, both parties suffer tangible costs. Psychological punishment may be inflicted by creating tension, uncertainty and loss of confidence at the conference table. The ability to punish or withhold reward goes hand-in-hand with the exercise of influence.

3. *BALANCE OF LEGITIMACY.* No other source of power is so hypnotic in its effect as legitimacy. We have learned to accept the authority of ownership, tradition, appointment and laws to such an extent that we *fail* to question their applicability in changing situations. It is the attack on legitimacy by militant blacks and whites that so disturbs our society. Legitimacy is a source and symbol of power.

For the buyer, legitimacy can be enhanced through laws, procedures, procurement regulations or review agencies such as fair-trade commissions. The government exerts influence through its elected role and through the media of public opinion and congressional investigation. A seller can enhance his legitimacy through institutional advertising, trade associations and political pressure. Even the seller's right to a fair profit and the buyer's right to a fair price have a legitimacy deeply rooted in our culture. In each case the principle is the same: the buyer, the seller and the government are building strength on the basis of higher institutional or cultural authority.

4. *BALANCE OF COMMITMENT.* Commitment, loyalty and friendship are benchmarks of power. Those with teenage children are aware that one of the strong bases of parental authority is associated with companionship rather than material rewards. Managers often learn that a mediocre worker who is committed to company objectives may be more effective than a talented but less dedicated man.

In a marriage, the party who cares most about maintaining the relationship gives up a degree of power to the party who is less committed. The commercial and diplomatic world do not differ in this respect. Purchasing executives have long realized that buyer and seller must be committed to each other's long-range interests if a satisfactory business relationship is to exist.

5. *BALANCE OF KNOWLEDGE.* Knowledge and the control of information is power. The more a negotiator knows about an opponent's objectives and bargaining position the stronger he is. Knowledge of product, marketplace, legal phraseology and regulations is also a source of strength. By the same token, a thorough understanding of the theory and practice of professional negotiation is an essential ingredient of power.

6. *BALANCE OF COMPETITION.* Competition has an important effect on bargaining power. The seller who can keep his plant busy on other work and the buyer with multiple sources are in a strong bargaining position.

Competition can also be created in other ways. A buyer may increase competition by bringing other economic forces into the transaction. For example, he can urge that the company make a product rather than buy it, or he can entice manufacturers from other fields into the marketplace. Sometimes an end product can be redesigned in order to eliminate dependency upon an exploitive vendor. Competition can be enhanced by providing funding, facilities, tooling and knowledge to otherwise marginal second-source suppliers.

A seller may improve his competitive position by developing a unique knowledge or facility base. He may also purchase other companies, which improves distribution channels and makes him less dependent upon specific customers or seasonal variations.

Last but not least, it is possible to improve one's competitive position by the simple expedient of selecting negotiators who are personally competitive: men who enjoy struggle and have a strong desire to win.

7. *BALANCE OF UNCERTAINTY AND COURAGE.* Security is a goal that humans cherish. We share a desire to avoid risk wherever possible. The person who is willing to accept a greater burden of uncertainty with respect to reward or punishment enhances his power.

Uncertainty may be based on fear and prejudice rather than rational grounds. For example, two of my friends are lawyers whose incomes have risen over a ten-year period from $15,000 to $45,000 a year. One is always fearful that next year's business will slip back to the $15,000 level. The other has faith in his future growth and generally negotiates higher fees. People assess risk differently even when they have access to the same information. A common stock which looks like a speculation to a man who lived through the depression can appear a sound investment to a young man. By the same token, I know some very intelligent people who lived through the real-estate decline of the thirties. They are still renting apartments in areas where land values have risen tenfold due to population pressures.

Some risks can be foreseen while others cannot. The owner of a machine shop estimates a tight tolerance job on the basis of a 10 percent scrap rate. His past experience with rejections on close tolerance work permits a rational estimate to be made. On the other hand, he cannot foresee that the internal structure of a particular batch of material will be too porous to hold the necessary dimensions.

Uncertainty can be created by introducing risk at a personal as well as corporate level. Deadlock introduces the possibility that a good negotiator can lose his reputation. Risk can be heightened by introducing matters in which the opponent's knowledge or ability to grasp a situation is deficient.

Courage plays a part in the decision to make a concession, to hold one's ground, or to force a deadlock. In personal injury work the insurance claims manager can never be sure that his low offer will precipitate costly litigation. Conversely, the claimant can only hope that a final verdict will justify his reluctance to accept an earlier offer. It takes courage to tolerate uncertainty, and we differ in our ability to do so.

8. *BALANCE OF TIME AND EFFORT*. Time and patience are power. The party that is most constrained by time limits provides the opponent with a base of strength. It is for this reason that purchasing executives stress the importance of lead time and early-warning inventory systems.

Buying, selling and negotiation are grueling work, and the willingness to work is power. Perhaps the hardest work of all is imposed on us by the demands of planning and deadlock. Both can easily be avoided: one by nonplanning and the other by agreement. The party most willing to work hard gains power. Some people are simply lazy and thereby forfeit this important source of strength.

9. *BALANCE OF BARGAINING SKILL*. Bargaining skill is power, and that's what this book is all about. The ability to plan, to persuade, to manipulate perceptions, to mobilize bias,

to analyze power and decision-making, to select effective people and to understand the theory and anatomy of negotiation constitutes a base of power available to buyer and seller alike. Can anyone afford to relinquish this source of strength?

PERCEIVING POWER

Power, notwithstanding its source, must be perceived if it is to exist. Two ingredients of perception are essential: the bargainer must know or think he has power while his opponent must believe that power exists and accept its authority. Figure 3 represents a concept of power that incorporates three elements: sources, perception and negotiation anatomy.

To perceive power objectively, it is not enough to simply ask, "How much power do I have in relation to my opponent?" The questions that should be asked fall into two categories:

A. Questions related to Negotiator's power:
   1. How does Negotiator perceive his own power?
   2. How does Negotiator believe that Opponent perceives Negotiator's power?
   3. How does Negotiator want Opponent to perceive Negotiator's power?

B. Questions related to Opponent's power:
   1. How does Negotiator perceive Opponent's power?
   2. How does Opponent perceive his own power?
   3. How does Opponent want Negotiator to perceive Opponent's power?

Perception plays a major role in creating bargaining power. The manager of a car agency remarked that the average buyer is his own worst enemy. There are many cars to choose from in Los Angeles, but buyers tend to fall in love with a specific model after shopping around for a few days. Once the choice is made, the buyer forfeits the advantages of a competitive market. An alert salesman perceives and exploits this shift in power by raising the price through extras. If the buyer stopped to analyze his perception of power prior to final agreement, he would be inoculated against lowballing and thereby avoid the purchase of high-priced extras, which were never wanted in the first place.

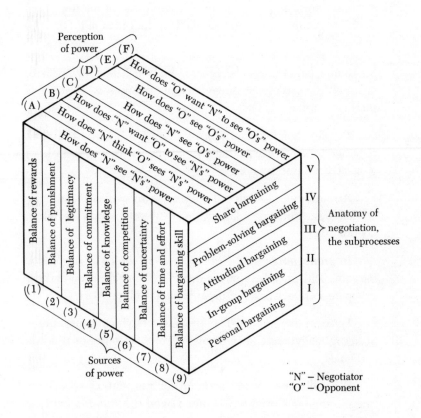

Figure 3. POWER AND PERCEPTION MODEL

THE ANATOMY OF NEGOTIATION

The model shown in Figure 3 indicates that power must be perceived in terms of five bargaining subprocesses. In Chapter 11 we will discuss the anatomy of negotiation in detail. At this point it is sufficient to indicate what is meant by each process and to point out that power must be analyzed in terms of each process individually. For example, power relationships exist and must be perceived in relation to the negotiator's own decision group (in-group) as well as in relation to the opponent.

Share bargaining–The process by which opponents share or ration the settlement range between themselves. If one gets more, the other gets less.

Problem-Solving–The process by which both parties work together to solve each other's problems. In this process both gain at the same time.

Attitudinal bargaining–The process by which a mutually workable attitudinal relationship is developed to facilitate negotiation.

In-group bargaining–The process by which a negotiator bargains with members of his own team and decision-making group to derive workable organizational objectives.

Personal bargaining–The process by which a negotiator makes a behavioral choice involving conflicting personal needs and goals.

We will refer to the anatomy of negotiation at various times in the book prior to Chapter 11 and the above definitions should prove adequate until then.

SIX POWER-BUILDING QUESTIONS

To understand the power structure and perceive it properly is fine but not enough. A negotiator must know how to manipulate power in his favor. A methodical approach to this problem is useful.

The six power-building questions below will permit a negotiator to search for a course of action designed to improve his base of power.

1. Can I enhance my base of power by taking an action I am not presently taking?

2. Can I enhance my base of power by permitting or forcing my opponent to take an action he is not presently taking?

3. Can I enhance my base of power by causing my opponent and myself to take an action together we are not presently taking?

4. Can I enhance my base of power by not taking an action I am presently taking?

5. Can I enhance my base of power by preventing my opponent from taking an action he is presently taking?

6. Can I enhance my base of power by preventing my opponent and myself from taking an action we are presently taking?

As an illustration of the fourth point, I am reminded of how the British increased their bargaining power with the Americans during the late fifties. They threatened to abandon their military bases in Southeast Asia unless we provided favorable trade and military concessions in Great Britain. The British thereby increased their power by threatening to stop taking an action we wished them to continue.

At this point in our analysis we have discussed the principles and sources of power. In addition, we have developed a framework by which power can be perceived, tested and manipulated. Attention will now be directed to four interesting aspects of power—namely, *no power, brinksmanship, focal points* and *irrationality*.

THE POWER OF NO POWER

We have good news for the negotiator who is always complaining that he has little power. There is power in possessing no power at all. Those with teenage children have encountered the no-power variation from time to time. Recently a neighbor grounded his son for cutting classes. By week's end the neighbor was completely frustrated because the boy had openly defied the rules of grounding. Soon the boy was restricted to quarters for one month and deprived of allowance and hi-fi privileges. The boy responded without anger; he merely walked out of the house. Several days later he was asked to return without any preconditions. The boy restored the balance of power to a favorable position by rejecting his parents and their rewards.

Beleaguered debtors can turn upon creditors on the basis of no-power power. I have seen debtors respond to harassment by offering creditors a choice between accepting 20¢ on the dollar or nothing at all through bankruptcy. Most creditors accept the 20¢.

The law is not unkind to suppliers who contract for tasks beyond the *state of the art*, nor does it fail to protect minors who sign installment contracts. Ask any man who has been exposed to a woman's tears whether there is power in no power.

THE POWER OF BRINKMANSHIP

"Brinkmanship" is a term used by John Foster Dulles when he was Secretary of State. His concept of diplomacy was based upon massive retaliation. If the Soviets started a fight, we in America would finish it regardless of the price. Needless to say, the policy is fraught with danger, for the price may be so high that both parties will be blown to smithereens for minor reasons.

Brinkmanship has a place in negotiation. It is a valid, albeit dangerous, way to alter the balance of power. To understand how it works, imagine two negotiators climbing down a slippery mountain in such a way that if one slips, the other also falls. The power of each party lies in its ability to control the destiny of the other. They face an uncertain future together. Each must cooperate or *both* pay a steep price.

Militant blacks use brinkmanship as a tactic when they threaten to burn down the city if demands for jobs and school improvements go unrealized. Neither the white nor black community have anything to gain from a fire or riot, but their destinies are sufficiently tied to cause the whites to pay attention to the demands.

In commercial negotiations the brinkmanship tactic can be very effective. When one party threatens another with third-party action if agreement is not reached by the established deadline, they are implying that the next step may cause both to go down the precipice together. Often businessmen would rather agree than reveal their records to juries or government investigating committees. Brinkmanship tactics affect the balance of power when one side is more reluctant than the other to accept risk.

THE POWER OF FOCAL POINTS

Power sometimes exists within the situation itself and has little to do with economic or social factors. It may have nothing to do with issues or demands, or even facts. Focal points are power. Let me explain.

There is a simplicity about certain common situations. If there are four people sharing a piece of pie, the host usually splits it in quarters. How else? The law recognizes that money acquired while a husband and wife live together must be shared equally. How else?

The magic of mathematical precision can be illustrated through a conflict faced by an old woman who knew that she was soon to die and wished to distribute $10,000 among her four children. One son earned a comfortable living from a good profession; the other was a struggling merchant with an insecure future. The elder daughter was married to a postman, who earned little; the younger earned a good salary as a secretary and showed little inclination toward marriage. The mother wrestled with the problem for six months before leaving each of her children $2,500, for she loved them equally. Another distribution probably would have made greater sense from a social standpoint.

Historical precedents operate in much the same way. The union finds it easier to settle with General Motors after Ford has reached an agreement. Similarly, if cost-accounting records indicate that a man can assemble eleven roller skates an hour, it becomes difficult to insist that a rate of fifteen is justified. The power of status quo is based upon the same principle. We may not be happy with things as they are, but if a pattern has been established we are prone to give it legitimacy.

Natural boundaries have powers of their own. The 38th Parallel in Korea is a natural place to split the country, for the map itself cries out, "If not here, where else?" In Vietnam we are not favored by a geographical focal point, but we use the political demilitarized zone in the same way. The power inherent in this arbitrary line was evidenced by the fact that both sides maintained the fiction despite intense battles within the zone itself.

Focal points play a part in establishing the power relationship between opponents. A good audit or cost-analysis is based upon mutually acceptable standards, whereas a poor report is less credible because it lacks standards. The skilled negotiator may be the one who has the ability to formulate issues in terms of favorable natural forces. For those who remain skeptical we ask: How many times have you reached an agreement by the simple expedient of splitting differences?

THE POWER OF IRRATIONALITY

It sometimes pays to be unreasonable and irrational in negotiation. A few years ago I negotiated with a most irrational man. My home needed painting, so I decided to get three local contractors to bid. After checking references I was convinced that the low bidder would do a good job. At contract-signing time he gave me a surprise. The painter refused to do the job unless paid in advance. Now, anyone with a bit of sense knows that it's foolish to give a contractor money in advance—especially so when the company is small. Yet the man insisted that this was the only way he would do business. Having been forced into a lengthy lawsuit five years earlier, he refused to open himself to that possibility again no matter what the credit rating of his customer. Furthermore, he pointed out that every customer paid him in advance and was perfectly satisfied, so why was I being unreasonable. To add credibility to his claim he permitted me to choose five names at random from his job-history book and check them myself. Wouldn't you know it, they all reported satisfaction with his work. I signed and got a good paint job—from this irrational man.

There is no iron law of nature that says a negotiator need be logical. Even with the best of intentions it is difficult to separate facts from the emotions, intuitions and assumptions that go into the interpretation process. Irrationality may be an appropriate tactic if the negotiator can 1) be sure that his

opponent understands what he can gain by reaching an agreement, and 2) can convince the opponent that he is *emotionally*
committed to the reasonableness of his "irrational" position.
The logical opponent who believes that the negotiator is emotionally committed will be forced into accepting some benefits
rather than none at all.

PSYCHOLOGICAL EXPERIMENTS IN POWER

Heretofore our attention has been focused upon those
factors of a structural nature that constitute the sources, perception and manipulation of power. The psychological aspects
that determine how an individual will be predisposed to look
at a power relationship have not been considered. There is
growing evidence that it is possible to predict how a person
will react to power.

Experimental research has, until recently, been rather
limited in the area of power and authority. A number of experiments are beginning to shed light on the subject.[11] In one
study the question was asked, "When high- and low-self-esteem
persons are given difficult tasks to do by a power figure, which
one feels more threatened?" The investigator concluded that
persons with low self-esteem feel more threatened by power
figures than those who have a higher regard for themselves.
This effect was particularly marked when the power figure provided clear instructions for the difficult task. When instructions
were given in a confusing manner, both felt threatened but the
effect tended to be more poignant for those with low self-
regard.

Equally important was the finding that high-worth individuals cope with frustrations imposed from above by working harder, persisting longer and by resisting the right of
authority to give unclear instructions. Persons with low self-
esteem showed a tendency to accept injustice passively. They

were also more concerned with maintaining good relations than fighting back.

Another experimenter discovered that *well-adjusted* persons, when placed in new situations, perceive relative power more *accurately* and are more effective in influencing group members than those who are not.

Expertise, knowledge and skill are related to feelings about power. It's logical that those who know more about a subject should feel more confident in influencing another to their viewpoint. But what happens when people merely think they know more than an opponent but in reality do not? Does the fact that they *think* they are experts affect their attitude toward power? Furthermore, what happens when the expert runs into an adversary who won't be influenced? Does he alter his perception of power?

These questions were asked by George Levinger in an exciting experiment involving a simulated city-planning conference between a designer and an associate. The designer proposed a design and was supposed to convince the associate of its merits. In all cases the associates were stooges of the investigator and were instructed to either reject or favor most points in the proposed plan. The designer was informed in advance that the associate was or was not an expert in city planning. The pairs then proceeded to discuss twenty-four decision points. Levinger measured: 1) the number of attempts to influence made by the designer, 2) the number of times the designer resisted influence and 3) the number of positive statements made by the designer about his own rights in the matter.

The investigator found that designers who were told in advance that an associate was an expert in city planning felt weaker initially and *continued* to be worried about resistance to their proposed ideas even when the associate evidenced a clear pattern of agreement. On the other hand, designers who considered themselves superior made more attempts to influence and were more assertive. The evidence seems clear that individuals who start with the belief that they have less power make fewer attempts to test reality. *They continue to underestimate their power even in the face of contrary evidence.*

Other investigations indicate that individuals with less relative power tend to be treated better by strong opponents than the ratio of their strength would normally indicate. My research confirmed that powerful men with skill are benevolent. There is evidence also that those with strength tend to overestimate its potency and are slow to react to less tangible sources of strength in adversaries. Perhaps President Johnson fell into this category with respect to North Vietnam.

It is well to remember that experimental research in power is in its infancy. This is particularly true with respect to bargaining power. On the other hand, the question of dominance and aggression has been of interest to psychiatrists since the turn of the century.

THE PSYCHOLOGY OF POWER

An infant is exposed to conflicts of power from birth as he attempts to achieve independence in a world that demands a degree of submission for every inducement it offers. As the child grows, efforts toward self-determination are enlarged first in the form of food selectivity and later in an effort to gain freedom from parental control. Each move toward independence involves a threatened loss of parental security. In adulthood the struggle for power is expanded to include outside persons and institutions.

The drive for self-determination results in attempts to influence other people and to achieve competence over tasks to be done. Success breeds increased self-esteem and a growing belief in one's power and competence over new situations.

Most psychologists agree that those who are insecure in their self-regard and anxious about their ability to control people or events become excessively concerned with achieving power. Children of authoritarian parents tend to place greater value on authority, tradition and discipline than those brought up in more permissive homes. They also tend to become authoritarian parents themselves. On the other hand they continue to seek the comforts of submission when faced with strong power figures. In short, they tend to demand structure when they have power and become submissive when they do not. Contrariwise, persons who are low in authoritarianism show little admiration for those in authority and reject attempts at influence. However, these are but generalizations and not necessarily applicable on an individual basis. Children of authoritarians sometimes reject their parents' values so completely that they move in the opposite direction.

The evidence is by no means clear or complete. We will nevertheless suggest a hypothesis that merits further research. Individuals appear to have a disposition to perceive power in a set pattern that dates back to early experience. We suggest that parents who permit a wide range of parent-child negotiation in early relationships and do not permit their children the luxury of easy victories will produce adults who are effective negotiators. These adults will be predisposed to resist undue influence and to show less respect for traditional power structures. Unfortunately, I know of no experiments or research that supports or rejects this hypothesis.

CONCLUSION

As our national wealth grows larger and society provides opportunity rather than mere survival to its poor, we will witness the growing impotence of raw power. Traditional sources of power, such as financial reward, punishment and competition are already less impressive than they were only a short while ago. Conventional symbols of authority are certain to suffer as our world moves away from survival values to an age of individuality and ideas.

When I went to college the sign DON'T WALK ON THE GRASS meant just that. I didn't reason it out precisely, but I had no doubt that the consequences of walking a block out of my way were less disturbing than facing some irate college policeman or administrator. I never questioned that somebody had carefully thought the matter out before putting up the sign.

Our children are approaching the matter differently. They look at the sign and the location of the school building to which they are going. If it doesn't make sense to them, they walk across the grass. Eventually some wise administrator decides that a winding concrete path might look well where the students have worn their way.

In business as well as in international relations, traditional power is under assault. Those of my generation (the over thirty-fives) are least able to cope with the new look of power. We grew up in an age where one followed the rules or faced lean years. Opportunities were not so prevalent then as now. Our generation takes too defeatist an attitude toward power. We tend to start by overestimating the power of our opponents and underestimating our own—especially where less tangible aspects of power are concerned.

Some years ago Dylan Thomas wrote a poem "Do Not Go Gentle into That Good Night." I would like to say to negotiators of my generation, "Don't Go Gently into the Day." You have more power than you think.

CHAPTER 6

MEN
WHO
INFLUENCE

IF YOU HAVE THE POWER OF UTTERING THE WORD, YOU
WILL HAVE THE PHYSICIAN AND TRAINER YOUR SLAVE,
AND THE MONEYMAKER WILL GATHER TREASURES, NOT
FOR HIMSELF, BUT FOR YOU WHO ARE ABLE TO SPEAK AND
TO PERSUADE THE MULTITUDE.

Plato

FOR ANY MEDIUM HAS THE POWER OF IMPOSING ITS OWN
ASSUMPTIONS ON THE UNWARY. BUT THE GREATEST AID
IS SIMPLY IN KNOWING THAT THE SPELL CAN OCCUR IM-
MEDIATELY UPON CONTACT, AS IN THE FIRST BARS OF A
MELODY.

Marshall McLuhan

I once had a tenant with the unlikely name of Bill Smith. A
tall, good-looking man in his mid-fifties, Bill's temples were
gray just where they were supposed to be. He spoke in a mild,
soft tone, almost songlike, and smiled a lot as the words came
out. The words themselves were logical rather than profound—
easy to understand. I never had a tougher tenant than Bill, or
one who could negotiate as well. Before terminating the lease

he convinced me to buy his rugs and fixtures at practically new prices. "After all," he argued, "are they not in exquisite taste?" They were, they were. He had a rare quality, and one wanted to believe him and please him.

Advertising men have discovered quite a lot about the art of influence in the process of driving us mad with television commercials. I often wonder whether more thought goes into the commercial than the program itself. We who negotiate can learn much from those whose profession it is to persuade, for they understand Bill Smith and those he influences.

If we are to understand persuasion, then it must be in a systematic way. Once the persuasion process is understood, we will find out how the personalities of opinion-changers and -nonchangers differ.

THE PERSUASION MODEL

A negotiation conference captures for a moment the business and personal life of its participants. It is a stage on which the players are both actor and audience. The *Persuasion Model* shown in Figure 4 is applicable to negotiation because it describes the process by which a communicator influences an audience.[12] It shows that the audience receives messages from four directions at once: the communicator, the subject matter, the media and the situation itself. The total message is then interpreted by the audience from a personal standpoint. If it is learned and accepted, change follows.

With this model in mind, we will consider each element of the influence process and its relationship to negotiation.

WHOM DO PEOPLE BELIEVE?

In "Fiddler on the Roof," Tevye, a poor milkman with five unmarried daughters, is depressed. As he daydreams about what it would be like to have money, his face lights up and he sings "If I Were a Rich Man." If he were a rich man, people would come to his home with wonderfully bewildering problems and wait patiently for his words of wisdom. It would not matter, he says, if he were right or wrong or even if they did not understand his answers. If he were rich, they would believe and go away content.

Tevye is talking about the credibility of a communicator.

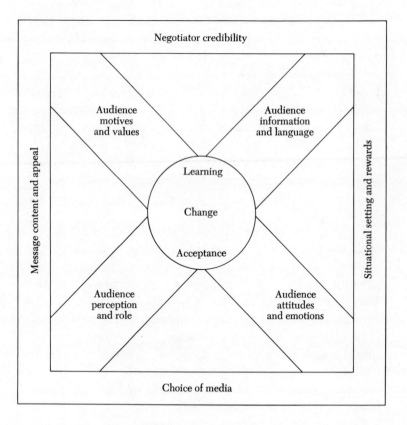

Figure 4. PERSUASION MODEL

Psychologists confirm that Tevye is right. When a communicator enjoys public status he is believed. A speaker's public image may be enhanced by his title, position, educational degree or wealth.

A man is believed if the listener considers him an expert and one to be trusted. In several studies it was found that opinion change was greater in response to a statement supposedly signed by a famous expert than an *identical* statement signed by an unknown person. Other studies indicate that speakers who are introduced in a way that leads the audience to consider them trustworthy are believed more readily than those not so introduced, *even when the message and speaker are the same.*[13]

Credibility does not always rest on a bed of substance. People who are good-looking, older and white enjoy greater influence than those who are not. People in high-status occupations are believed more readily than those doing ordinary work. When an individual is believed in one subject area there is a tendency to believe him in another. Fortunately, this transferability has limits, for we still have enough common sense to separate the ideas of General LeMay, soldier, from General LeMay, politician.

From a negotiation standpoint the need for credibility is clear. We must enhance the credibility of the negotiation team in every way possible. There is no reason to introduce competent engineers with distinguished patents merely as "Mr. Jones, our engineer." Yet, this is typically what happens in a negotiation. It makes good sense to bring to the attention of one's opponent the past experience, accomplishments and special qualifications of team members. Needless to say, discretion in doing so is necessary.

A negotiator who has done his homework and has an intimate knowledge of products, markets, regulations and issues is likely to appear credible to an opponent—ignorance and laziness have a way of showing. Trust can be developed by reference to past dealings that have worked out well or by the performance of small or large promises prior to and during the conference. In any case, the question of credibility should not be left to chance but should be carefully nurtured.

MESSAGE (WHAT DID YOU SAY?) CONTENT AND APPEAL

Everything that goes on in a negotiation is a message, including the conference itself. A message may consist of commitments, threats, moves and questions as well as nonverbal elements. The following headlines from Vietnam are to the point:

SAIGON REFUSES TO PARTICIPATE IN TALKS
Message: Saigon is independent of the United States

VIET CONG THROWS BIG PARTY IN SWANK HOTEL
Message: The NLF exists and has money

SAIGON DOESN'T LIKE SHAPE OF TABLE
Message: Some factions are more equal than others

SAIGON WILL NOT ADDRESS VIET CONG AT TABLE
Message: They do not exist until we say they do

36-HOUR TRUCE—14 AMERICAN POW'S RETURNED
Message: Hanoi will respond if bombing stops

More will be said about the verbal and nonverbal content of communication in Chapter 14. It is pertinent here to consider recent research findings regarding the best way to make a message carry persuasive impact. The suggestions below are based upon experimental evidence accumulated in the recent past.[14]

1. It is more effective to present both sides of an issue.

2. When the pros and cons of an issue are being discussed it is better to present the communicator's favored viewpoint last.

3. Listeners remember the beginning and end of a presentation more than the middle.

4. Listeners remember the end better than the beginning, particularly when they are unfamiliar with the argument.

5. Conclusions should be explicitly stated rather than left for the audience to decide.

6. Repetition of a message leads to learning and acceptance.

7. A message that first arouses a need and then provides information to satisfy it is remembered best. However, when a need-arousal message is threatening, the listener has a tendency to reject it.

8. When two messages must be delivered, one of which is desirable to the audience and the other undesirable, the most desirable should come first.

9. A message that asks for the greatest amount of opinion-change is likely to produce the most change. Here, as in other aspects of life, aspiration level is related to success.

10. Learning and acceptance are improved if stress is placed on similarities of position rather than differences.

11. Agreement is facilitated when the desirability of agreement is stressed.

12. Agreement on controversial issues is improved if they are tied to issues on which agreement can easily be reached.

In addition to these specific findings, students of human behavior have discovered through clinical evidence and keen observation that people who place others on the defensive do not succeed in convincing them. People who belittle the opinions of others, are argumentative and always reflect sureness about their own viewpoint make their opponents hostile. Those who bring friendliness and sympathy to the table, request advice from the opponent and appeal to his higher motives for fairness, worth and excellence have a better chance of changing the opponent to their way of thinking.

Opinions are in many ways like personal possessions. People react violently to being assaulted and robbed, but will often be responsive to those whose needs are made clear and whose claims are rational.

THE MEDIA AND THE MESSAGE

Sir Francis Bacon addressed himself to the question of media in his essay "Of Negotiation," written in 1608. He said:

> It is generally better to deal by speech than by letter; and by mediation of a third person than by a man's self. Letters are good, when a man would draw an answer by letter back again; or when it may serve for a man's justification afterwards to produce his own letter; or where it may be dangerous to be interrupted; or heard by pieces. To deal in person is good, when a man's face breedeth regard as commonly with inferiors; or in tender cases, where a man's eye upon the countenance of him with whom he speaketh may give him a direction how far to go; and generally, where a man will reserve to himself liberty either to disavow or expound.

Bacon's advice makes sense even today. It is still generally better to face an opponent than to deal by letter or telephone. Third-party mediators continue to facilitate agreement just as they did in Bacon's day. His exceptions are as valid today as they were then because the choice of media cannot be separated from questions of documentation, evidence, physical appearance and information-control.

Media is closely related to the credibility of facts. Communication channels provide authority to messages. A financial article in the *Wall Street Journal* on interest rates is believed more readily than one in the *Newark News*. A cost standard derived from properly kept accounting records is more credible than one developed by analysis. Books of account, formal procedures, regulations and computer-tab runs are media in the same sense as are newspapers and television.

A choice of media is always available in negotiation. We can choose to use visual aids, volumes of written documentation, scratch notes or a carefully produced movie film to present a viewpoint. A message may be conveyed in the secrecy of a Paris cocktail party or in the glare of world television. Marshall McLuhan said, "the medium is the message." Certainly the content of a message is shaped by the channel through which it is delivered.

The same message may be rejected in one social setting but accepted in another. My wife, normally an agreeable person, is impervious to any message that precedes her first cup of coffee. In negotiation the proper setting may include such factors as meeting place, time of day, hotel accommodations, shape of table and distance from home. Even such matters as Christmas holidays and the Fourth of July can influence the course of a negotiation. I know a buyer who tries to arrange negotiation conferences for late Friday afternoons. He is convinced that a better deal can be made at that time because supplier representatives are anxious to get away for the weekend.

Media is a matter of choice. There is no guarantee that the correct media for a message will develop without forethought. It probably won't. With respect to situational setting we usually have more choice than we think. There is no reason to accept categorically the location, time, creature comforts and general rules for a negotiation. The situational setting is itself a negotiable issue.

THE AUDIENCE

Most complex negotiations involve more than one person on each side. It is no longer possible for one person to be adept at technical matters, law, accounting and economics. This is true of the retail buyer as well as the industrial buyer. In aerospace negotiations the problems are incredibly complex and the zone of uncertainty so large that opposing teams consist of engineers, pricing specialists and auditors to assist the team captain. These men constitute the audience in a negotiation. On the surface they appear to be of one mind. But as likely as not their unanimity of purpose is apt to prove more vulnerable than it looks.

The team members are individuals with both common and divergent interests. Despite the procedural dictum stating that the buyer is the leader, the real leader may well be the engineer. The team members are not equal in status or in authority. To complicate matters still further, the audience also includes interested parties back home.

The real-estate salesman makes it his business to recognize the needs of prospective home-buying families in terms of their individual motives. The good points of a home are described so that each member's wants are aroused and his fears allayed. The salesman knows that a negotiation will take place back home, so he wants each family member to work on the other in his behalf.

In the *Persuasion Model*, seven audience factors are shown. A negotiator who wants to persuade his opponent must consider each factor from an individual as well as team standpoint. He must give thought to audience perception, information, attitudes, motives, language, values and roles. In addition he should keep two points in mind. First, an audience responds to messages that provide rewards. They like communications that reinforce personal or group opinions, and they enjoy listening to information that makes them feel worthwhile. On the other hand, they become hostile to messages that represent a threat to status or security. Second, people like balance in their lives and perceptions. If they like John and Mary, they are uncomfortable if John dislikes Mary. If they are smart they are uncomfortable with being poor. If they are important at work, they are disturbed by an office setting that does not reflect their importance. Ambiguity and imbalance create tension in an audience. Uncertainty of any kind, whether due to the unpredictability of nature or the lack of adequate information, also creates tension. This feeling of unease can be an opportunity for the man intent upon persuading an opponent, for there is a human tendency to reduce ambiguity and uncertainty as quickly as possible. Many prefer closure at almost any price rather than face the anxieties that accompany protracted indecision or deadlock.

An analysis of the opponent's team structure from the standpoint of audience reaction can facilitate opinion-change. Learning and acceptance are improved when a message is tailored for the listener. If a message fails to take account of the social forces at work, or of the facts, methods, goals and values of the audience, it is likely to fall on deaf ears.

LEARNING, ACCEPTANCE AND CHANGE

Change can occur only if a message is learned and accepted. The learning process involves hearing and understanding. Acceptance implies that the person feels the information is relevant and likes the idea. A listener must have enough intelligence to learn and enough motivation to accept if his decision behavior is to be changed.

Most of us have wondered why there are people who can

be sold almost anything. Psychologists explain this type as one whose ability is adequate for learning and evaluation but who has an unusually strong motive to *visualize* himself actually using the product. Vacuum-cleaner salesmen know that there are women who are self-driven to buy expensive cleaners with gadgets they will never use. They persuade themselves.

One purpose of negotiation is to influence an opponent to change his decision behavior in favor of the negotiator's viewpoint. While we cannot be content merely with changes in opinion, sentiment or perception, such changes are nevertheless important, for they are prerequisites to behavior change. People tend to behave in ways that are consistent with their opinions.

Having looked at the elements that make up the persuasion process, we are in a better position to direct attention to the personality differences between people who change opinions and those who do not. A message that is delivered with skill and understanding can change the viewpoint of even the most hardened influence-resister. A gullible man, on the other hand, needs little prompting to change his mind.

THE PERSONALITY OF CHANGERS AND NONCHANGERS

Some of us are gullible and others are not. I know executives at work who nod their heads in agreement to almost everything they hear. There are people who cannot resist buying what others have to sell. Some are Democrats today, Republicans tomorrow, and Democrats the day after on the basis of little more than paid political announcements. If, in the course of negotiation, you run into a gullible opponent, be grateful and win graciously.

What is the difference between an opinion-changer and -nonchanger? Probably, *self-esteem is the most important factor.* Persons who think well of themselves are less vulnerable to opinion-change and less susceptible to influence than persons who do not.

Individuals who have a good self-image *initiate* attempts to influence, *reject* influence and believe that they are more influential than those who see themselves in a lesser light. A substantial number of studies agree that low-self-esteem persons are *persuasible*, feel inadequate under pressure and do not assert themselves.

The relationship of self-esteem to persuasibility was clearly seen in the case of a man I once worked for. When I first met him, he had recently been promoted to vice-president and was scared. What made matters worse was that his predecessor had done the same job exceedingly well.

In the early months the new man took advice from everybody. He listened carefully to old friends and associates, and many of his early decisions were based on the advice of these well-meaning people. For about a year I was assigned to a remote location and we lost touch with each other, but I heard rumors that he was gaining acceptance among those on top. When we met again the change was obvious. It was not that he looked well, dressed better or had his office appointed in good taste. All this was true, but in a sense only symbolic of something else, the flavor of which was captured by a chance remark. He said, "You know, I've learned in this job that my ability is better than that of most of the people who give me advice. It took me a year to figure out that I have this job and they don't because I have better judgment." I left without a word of counsel. It took the "Bay of Pigs" to teach a similar lesson to President John F. Kennedy. Self-esteem is very closely related to persuasibility. There are, however, other critical factors.

Two investigators conducted a series of experiments with a group of people classified by psychological tests as changers and nonchangers.[15] The subjects were then given a battery of seven tests in an effort to recognize personality differences. Let us see how they differed.

In one test the subject and a stooge of the experimenter were seated in a dark room. A light beam was projected on the wall and then moved. The confederate attempted to influence the subject regarding the amount of movement. *Nonchangers* formed their own basis for judging the amount of movement; changers did not. In a perceptual test involving orientation to a tilting chair and hidden figures in a drawing, *changers* were less aware of subtle differences in their physical and visual world than *nonchangers.*

Three questionnaires were administered. The first tested whether subjects were inner-directed or outer-directed. They found that *changers* had a strong need for social approval, security and conformity while *nonchangers* were concerned with self-expression, creative striving and achievement. Changers focused their thoughts on people while nonchangers were concerned with ideas and principles. The second questionnaire tested whether the subjects were authoritarian or not. *Changers* were harsh in their condemnation of social deviates, tended to reject new ideas and admired people in power. *Nonchangers* were more accepting and had little admiration for power. In the third test the investigators confirmed that nonchangers thought more highly of themselves.

The final two tests explored the subjects' fantasy world. In a figure-drawing exercise changers drew weak, dependent male figures that lacked sexual features. Nonchangers made stronger male figures with sensual and sexual characteristics. A Rorschach test was administered and revealed that changers have a passive self-image, lack imagination and are not critical of themselves or others. Nonchangers, on the other hand, were assertive, analytical, creative and evaluative.

Two other variables appear to predispose people toward being easily influenced. One is a high need for social approval; the other is an inability to tolerate uncertainty and ambiguity.

Research indicates that those with high tolerance levels tend to withstand persuasion attempts. Paradoxically, those who lack intelligence are often closed-minded to persuasion because they fail to understand what is being said. Perhaps this is why Sir Francis Bacon recommended the use of "absurd men for business that doth not bear out itself."[16]

On the basis of these and other investigations we may conclude that the personality traits of a nonchanger are high self-esteem, inner-directedness, tolerance of ambiguity, high assertiveness, low authoritarianism and a low level of anxiety.

CONCLUSION

A total planning concept of negotiation must include systematic planning in persuasion. While it is true that some people are intuitively good at persuading others, for most of us the most reliable path to success lies in knowing what we want to achieve and systematically deciding how we want to go about it. The persuasion model was designed to help those of us whose intuition is less than perfect.

There is an old Rumanian curse, "May you have a brilliant idea which you know is right and be unable to convince others." In the last analysis, the art of convincing others consists of saying and doing those things that cause others to *want to do* what you want them to do. The viewpoints presented in this chapter cannot assure success: there is no guarantee that one's ideas will be accepted by his opponent. Without these new tools of persuasion, however, things will go more poorly than they should.

CHAPTER 7

INOCULATION
AGAINST
INFLUENCE

THIS ANIMAL IS VERY MISCHIEVOUS; WHEN IT IS ATTACKED, IT DEFENDS ITSELF.

Anonymous

Can men be inoculated against influence? On the basis of a series of ingenious experiments, William J. McGuire, psychologist, believes they can.[17] In this chapter we will learn what he discovered and how it can be applied to the real world of negotiation.

A biologist creates immunity by pre-exposing the patient to weakened doses of virus. The patient develops resistance that later enables him to withstand a real attack. McGuire reasoned that he could inoculate people with various defenses to influence and observe which defense was best able to withstand persuasion. His plan was simple: 1) find ideas that everybody believes in, 2) provide the believer with good reasons for his belief, 3) attack the belief and 4) measure opinion-change.

It isn't easy to find ideas in which everyone believes, but there are some. Certain beliefs are so rarely questioned that most men accept them at face value. Among these are such truisms as: "It's a good idea to brush your teeth after every meal if at all possible"; "Mental illness is not contagious"; and "Everyone should get a yearly chest X-ray to detect signs of TB at an early stage." McGuire prepared to challenge these ideas in a systematic way.

Subjects were divided into three groups. One group received a defense treatment that provided it with reasons *supporting* the belief. The second was allowed to develop *reasons against the belief and counterarguments* offsetting those reasons. The third was given a double defense—that is, the "supportive" approach of the first combined with the "negative" approach of the second.

After pretreatment, each belief was exposed to massive attack and opinion-change measured. Here is what McGuire found:

1. The double defense given the third group proved most effective. A belief is best reinforced when a) the believer develops arguments in favor of it, and b) practices offsetting the arguments of those who do not believe in it.

2. The second defense was next best. When a believer practices offsetting the arguments of disbelievers, he develops immunity.

3. The least effective defense, by far, was one in which the believer merely gave himself good reasons for supporting his opinion without any regard to the opinions of disbelievers. However, even this "supportive" defense was found to be much better than no defense at all.

4. The best way to improve any defense was to assure that the person participated actively in its development.

5. The greater the number of arguments in any defense the greater was the degree of inoculation achieved.

6. All defense treatments became less effective over time. Those in which the believer took no active part and those

which merely provided supporting arguments decayed most rapidly.

7. Resistance against influence was not greatest immediately after treatment but several days later. As in biological immunization, some time passes before the serum takes effect. Apparently, people have to digest arguments before they can use them.

It is evident from McGuire's findings that some ways of developing resistance are far better than others and that *any* defense is better than none. To the man who wishes to negotiate from a position of strength the implications are clear: inoculate, or pay the price for failing to do so.

PERSONALITY—THE BUILT-IN INOCULATOR

A man's personality may have a good deal to do with his ability to resist or not resist persuasion. Probably the best built-in defense is an effective ego and a high level of self-esteem. People who regard themselves highly and have an understanding of their own values, needs and abilities are not easily diverted from their goals.

Intelligence may also contribute to resistance, but its workings are less predictable. Intelligent people can evaluate an opponent's proposal before they accept his argument. However, if the opposing argument is sound, this can have the effect of producing opinion-change where none is desired.

A person's level of anxiety can contribute to his ability to resist persuasion. Anxious people *reject* new information that is threatening. While this is true of most people, those who are anxiety-ridden see danger everywhere. I know an accountant who insists that all work—no matter how small—done on his house by contractors be written into a contract. He simply refuses to believe anything unless it is put down on paper.

Motivation is a rather good predictor of resistance. It acts as a built-in inoculator. When a man is highly motivated to reach a goal, he is less likely to digress. There is always the danger, however, that such a man will fail to recognize a practical compromise in his zeal to optimize his objectives.

We may conclude that the traits most likely to provide resistance are self-confidence, aggressiveness, motivation and, in most cases, intelligence. Those traits least likely to convey resistance are dependency, indecisiveness, anxiety, defensiveness, social insecurity, hypersensitivity, feelings of inferiority and a lack of assertiveness.

BEHAVIORAL COMMITMENT

As important as personality is, it is no guarantee of success. When a negotiator commits himself to a course of action he immunizes himself against opinion-change. In effect he says, "If I change my opinion, I will have to suffer loss of self-worth or love from others."

A commitment may be made simply by making a decision. The act of deciding that a belief is worth holding provides stability to the belief. People who decide for themselves have a better chance to live by their standards than those who are forced to comply. This concept of commitment based upon free choice appears to apply as readily to negotiation as it does to psychotherapy.

Another way to make a commitment is to announce what you intend to do in public. (We will see later how a major company uses this technique to inoculate its negotiators.) President Nixon, in his early press conferences, was very careful to *avoid* hardening his overall position on Vietnam when asked about Hanoi's shelling of Saigon. He merely said that an appropriate response would be made. On the other hand, Hitler convinced Chamberlain of his intention to make war when he announced over the radio that he would fight if his demands were unmet. Both were aware of the importance of public statements in negotiation.

There is a purchasing manager who makes use of this principle in a practical way. Although a buyer is normally designated chief negotiator, the manager sometimes places the price analyst in charge when the buyer insists that he cannot make a deal at the price proposed by the analyst. The fact that the analysts have made a public announcement that the target price be set at a low level is sufficient to inspire them to a strong performance at the bargaining table.

Action taken in behalf of an opinion strengthens that opinion. McGuire found that persons who took an active part in a defense maintained their beliefs. We may likewise expect the buyer who defends his price objective to management to resist an opponent's attack on that objective.

The idea of behavioral commitment is not new to negotiation. The handwritten memorandum of agreement at the close of a conference has prevented many a man from having second thoughts the next morning. The act of putting down a deposit is usually enough to assure that a buyer will return to consummate an agreement. Sometimes a commitment to buy is revealed by the simple process of stating an offer. That is why car salesmen and real-estate brokers try so hard to get a prospect to make an offer.

ANCHORING BELIEFS TO VALUES

This technique might be called the *Domino Theory* of beliefs: if one falls, they all fall. When a goal can be tied to an important business principle or practice, it becomes hard to dislodge.

For example, the vice-president of an aggressive company advised me that he instructs purchasing management to squeeze every penny it can from the supplier. Every buyer knows that a fair and reasonable agreement is *not* the objective of this company. The old expression *"Let the buyer beware"* represents its buying and selling philosophy. All negotiation objectives are anchored to this tough-minded outlook.

On the other hand, the government and many aerospace contractors believe that the essence of good business is cooperation and fairness within a well-regulated framework. These people seek equity in every transaction rather than exploitation. However, there is some danger in this policy. Current research indicates that fair-minded players are themselves exploited when they encounter competitive opponents unless they also become competitive.

Another common way to implant opposition to influence is by associating bargaining objectives with budgetary goals. A buyer or seller who is aware of dollar bogies is likely to respond to this constraint. In the aerospace industry we occasionally bid foolishly and are forced to minimize losses by superior organization and dedication. One method that has proved useful is to put together a "tiger team" responsible for getting the job done economically. It is not unusual for a team to set bogies that appear ridiculously low in the light of past history. To the surprise of all, however, these targets are often achieved. The team's ability to oppose supplier influence appears to be related to the importance of the bogy.

We are all familiar with fear as an inoculator. A buyer who is threatened with dismissal unless he meets a target will be oblivious to the opponent's arguments. The businessman operating on a shoestring faces a similar threat. Fear inoculates against persuasion, but may also inoculate against decision-making of any kind.

Some managers believe that a negotiation team must be "fired up" to win, so they try to cultivate aggressiveness in the team's thinking. In our experiment, skilled negotiators with power were benevolent. Perhaps they would have been less so if we had made them aggressive by raising their aspiration level. Induced aggressiveness is, however, a dangerous technique because it may force the negotiation into an unnecessary deadlock. In the hands of an unskilled negotiator without power, it may merely spur the opponent on to greater efforts.

Company policy, bogies, fear and aggressiveness are but four ways in which resistance to opinion-change can be improved. Other methods such as training, loyalty, planning and knowledge of the negotiation process itself can also contribute in a direct fashion. In one major American corporation, buyers are immunized by procedure. The method is applicable to small and large businesses alike.

BUILDING IMMUNITY AT A GIANT CORPORATION

Buyers at the North American–Rockwell Corporation are required by directive to prepare a written plan *prior* to negotiations in excess of $125,000. The plan encompasses the following points:

1. Reasons for source selection.
2. Past procurement history.
3. Detailed analysis by a pricing specialist.
4. Detailed recommendations by the buyer regarding target prices, upper price limits and delivery.
5. Special requirements imposed by the prime contract or the product itself.

In addition, the directive provides that differences of opinion between team members regarding objectives be surfaced and explained. *The final plan requires high-level approval and cannot be changed without specific written authority.*

In requiring a strong behavioral commitment on the part of the buyer and his team, the policy has much to commend it. If the directive were to be expanded along the lines suggested by McGuire's research, it would be a more powerful document. Nevertheless, the company has left other aerospace firms behind in this respect.

CONCLUSION

Building resistance to persuasion is important work that can be done correctly—or for that matter left undone. In my experience it is usually done superficially. The Catholic Church introduced the idea of the "Devil's Advocate" centuries ago, but business has yet to adopt the concept on a workaday basis.

The usual arguments against inoculation are sound: there isn't enough time or talent available; and the nature of the negotiation process itself develops new information that makes many of the counterarguments less useful than their economic cost warrants. These are indeed important considerations and cannot be shrugged off lightly.

In negotiation *the process is the product,* and inoculation plays a key role in that process. Aside from its benefits at the table, a well-organized inoculation effort will reveal the risks inherent in the major issues. It will surface and question strategic goals and values. It will test the degree of intensity with which goals are held and the logic of alternative trade-offs. It will help define strategy in operational terms. It will force management to participate where it would often prefer to sit back and hope for the best.

These are benefits internal to the organization. From an external standpoint, the difference between average performance and good performance may well be inoculation. What is necessary is a commitment to the idea that one cannot prepare adequately for negotiation without it. In this as in other matters, it is what we value and aspire to that greatly determines our performance.

CHAPTER 8

STATUS

YOU! SAID THE CATERPILLAR CONTEMPTUOUSLY. WHO
ARE YOU?

Lewis Carroll

IN AMERICA, YOU ARE WHAT YOU DO.

Daniel P. Moynihan

Some years ago an officer told me about an Air Force training film on negotiation in which one team was led by a
colonel and the other by a major. He chuckled as he recalled
that every serviceman in that room knew who would win. Is
it possible in real life that we give the benefit of the doubt to
the colonel?

Human behavior can be analyzed from the standpoint of
social relationships such as status, role and group action. In
this chapter we will be concerned with *status*, which is defined
by Webster's as "a position or rank in relation to others." It's
fun to talk of status because all of us are involved with it.

ANIMAL STATUS SYSTEMS

Dominance systems exist in animal as well as human organizations. Most of us are familiar with the pecking habits

of hens. At first we are not aware of any order, but as individual hens are identified their pecking habits become visible and we find that not every hen pecks another. Between every two hens, one pecks and the other doesn't; one rules and the other submits. There is a clear order of dominance in the barnyard.

Higher-order animals share this trait. Dominance relationships develop when animals share an area or compete for food. When a conflict arises, one or the other gives up. Grizzlies dominate black bears, who dominate wolves. Animals with high status have precedence over food supplies, mates and territory.

How do animals settle status differences? Unlike man, they rarely fight. Instead, the winner is selected on his ability to put on a better show of power by pushing, roaring or snarling. The bark, not the bite, determines the contest. One naturalist described animal dominance as a "social guillotine," an unwritten agreement to share the wealth from the top down. When provisions are in short supply, those below are expected to move away, leaving to the higher members sufficient resources to survive.

HUMAN SYSTEMS

Status acts as a social guillotine among men. I have noticed over the years that layoffs in industry rarely affect those on top. Social class is related to resource allocation in man as in beast.

We are fond of thinking that the United States is a classless society. Nothing could be further from the truth. Despite the fact that people can move from class to class, we are as conscious of status here as any people on the globe. Everybody has a place on the pyramid and knows it.

At the turn of the century, Thorstein Veblen[18] developed a status theory that is still a cornerstone in modern marketing.

In earlier times warlords seized women and property as symbols of power. As civilization progressed and wealth was inherited, it became respectable to display one's power without fighting: by owning property and living up to a standard unattainable to others.

There were three avenues by which people could display high status: wealth, women and waste. The first way was to stop working for money altogether. The better classes soon began to devote energy to such conspicuous *nonproductive* activities as fox-hunting. Hunting for foxes soon gave way to hunting for public office: today's vocation for the truly rich.

Historically, wives worked in the fields to build the husband's economic strength. Later, as a sign of wealth, they were encouraged to live lives of elegant luxury. Their dress and manners became more ornate and functionally useless as their symbolic value grew. When women got the vote in 1920, a new trend developed. Rich women moved out of the home into social service with a vengeance. Thanks perhaps more to Eleanor Roosevelt than any other woman, a generation of American girls took their rightful places in industry, commerce and social work.

Today in America we see a resurgence of the original role of women. The wife no longer works in the field or enjoys useless leisure. She is instead a professionally trained college graduate ready, willing and able to cope with the rigors of business, social and household demands. Modern man clings to respectability by insisting that his wife works because she wants to. Once the family grows accustomed to the second paycheck, both husband and wife begin to silently wonder how they ever got along without it. The important thing is that they may seldom admit it to each other.

When Veblen wrote his book it was still easy to show how rich you were. Men like Diamond Jim Brady lived like potentates. They exuded wealth from every muscle. Big estates, big carriages, yachts, money, huge serving staffs and tremendous parties made the rich different from everybody else. In the depression years the rich found that discretion was the better part of ostentation. It became a good deal wiser to avoid unnecessary display while millions were unemployed. This trend continues to the present day. Wealth is not as easy to see as it once was. Only a few, like Aristotle Onassis or J. Paul Getty, have the desire to advertise their riches on a grand scale.

There is still one good way to prove that you are really wealthy, and that is by throwing money away. At the turn of the century, conspicuous consumption consisted of private railroad cars and huge yachts. Today the symbols of waste are a bit more subtle, consisting of boats that are rarely used, expensive mansions that are empty and chauffeurless Rolls-Royces carrying kids to expensive private schools. Wealth, women and waste continue to be the three foundation stones upon which status in America is built.

Veblen predicted that Americans would continue to imitate the tastes of the very rich. We have only to look at television to see that his theory has not been lost. In fact we are developing new ways of measuring status that might have surprised Veblen.

EMERGING SYMBOLS

As the twentieth century draws to a close, modern status symbols have emerged. First, there is the diploma elite. The college diploma has split the middle class into two groups: those who hold prestige jobs and those who do not. And now even the diploma-holders are threatened by the emergence of an army of computer-based men, mathematical management scientists, with doctorates. So the present-day manager is uneasy in the face of a technology he is unprepared for.

Modern financing methods and American economic stability have combined to produce a great many landowners. The house has re-emerged as a prime status symbol reinforced by gold bathroom fixtures, spiral staircases, crystal chandeliers and thirty-year expandable mortgages.

At the same time, easy credit and technology have reduced the importance of the horse-driven and horseless carriage. We are now in an era of *conspicuous nonconspicuousness* in this regard. The other day I saw a small foreign car that attracted my interest. When I spoke to the owner he couldn't wait to tell me that it cost $7,500. I walked away impressed but disturbed. After all, I was shopping for a compact car and this car was just compact enough in all but one respect.

In an affluent society it is becoming commonplace for middle-class families to join clubs for golf, tennis and yachting. Since one club name and letterhead looks much like another, one needs a scorecard for ranking clubs. The same is true of private schools. With the deterioration of the central city, men have been driven to find better educational facilities for their children. The trouble is that the middle class is new at the private-school status game and still confuses good education with fancy old names. One Westwood private institution, in a magnificent display of one-upmanship, advertises that it will accept only those children with IQ's of over 135. Even the waiting list has status.

Religious institutions have not escaped the modern search for position. It is better to be an Episcopalian than a Presbyterian, both of whom outrank Methodists, Catholics and Jews, in that order. I am told that Reform Jews outrank Conservative Jews, who stand above Orthodox Jews. I suppose it depends upon who is doing the ranking.

The beauty of status is that there is almost nobody who does not outrank somebody else. What made the movie "Charly" so poignant was that Charly outranked nobody, not even Algernon, the mouse. In our society, everybody has a place. Those on the bottom of the ladder are still trying to imitate those on top. Nowhere is this more evident than in the world of work.

STATUS IN THE WORK WORLD

"In America you are what you do." Occupation is the key to status. Essentially there appears to be five occupational classes. Into which do you fit?

I. Medical specialists, prominent scientists, top-level corporate executives, Wall Street lawyers, general staff officers, federal judges.

II. General practitioners, editors, engineers, local judges, local lawyers, professors and local business executives of large firms.

III. Bankers, purchasing agents, technical sales representatives, teachers, small to medium businessmen.

IV. Insurance men, retail managers, army enlisted personnel.

V. Skilled, semiskilled and unskilled workers, respectively.

While Americans are by no means agreed that these classes are accurately represented, they are reasonably aware of their own rank. Men have a tendency to rate those with whom they are acquainted and thereby develop an image of their own position in the occupational pyramid.

The organizational class system is known to all who work for large companies. In fact nobody is permitted to forget it even for a moment. A few observations about class structure in the aerospace industry are to the point.

Engineers have more status than administrative personnel. And among engineers, those who deal in abstractions such as systems engineering rank above those who design hardware. Among administrative groups, those who meet with important people have more status than those who deal with just anybody. This is why contract administrators tend to rank higher than subcontract administrators, despite the fact that both do essentially the same work.

Line personnel has more status than staff or service. The only exception to this occurs when a staff function possesses knowledge that the line *knows* it does not possess and cannot easily acquire. In that respect the most prestigious staff activities are concerned with law, economics, investment analysis, science and computers.

To the outside world a buyer is a buyer. Not so in big-company purchasing departments. Major subcontract administrators rank higher than those who buy moderately complex articles. General buyers and small buyers follow in that order.

Managers are supposed to be equal, but some are more "equal" than others. The engineering manager has greater status than the purchasing manager, who in turn outranks the price-analysis manager. Furthermore, it is not uncommon to see a design-engineering supervisor with more status than a purchasing manager. And purchasing people recognize this class distinction, for a buyer of engineering products is accorded greater esteem than one who buys operating supplies.

Status systems exist everywhere, and one need not be a sociologist to be aware of them. Some time ago I attended a negotiation in which a subcontract buyer faced two conglomerate vice-presidents with national reputations. The subcontract buyer practically gave the store away to his opponents. If the buyer's management had given but a few seconds' thought to the matter of status, a more equitable agreement might have resulted.

One can argue that the vice-presidents did not know the rank of their adversary, for, rest assured, the buyer went to no pains to advertise. I must disagree, because a man's rank is written all over his corporate face and is expressed in terms of job title, office size, location, office appointments, carpeting, executive typewriters, company cars and private dining room.

Status symbols are as obvious to executives as military insignia to an officer.

One may still ask, "What difference does all this really make in negotiation?" Research indicates that it makes quite a difference.

EXPERIMENTAL FINDINGS

We can best see how status works if we look at it through the viewpoint of self-worth. A person's status is intimately associated with what he thinks of himself. It is hard to assign oneself to a position of low rank and yet enjoy high self-esteem.

Investigators have discovered that those with low status introduce "job-irrelevant" subjects when speaking to their bosses. On the other hand, those with high status initiate "job-directed" talk. In another study, half the people were given reason to feel they ranked high and the other half low. The investigators found that lows have a stronger need to send messages to highs than vice-versa. However, on a social basis it is the highs who initiate invitations to dinner, suggest first-name relationships, borrow combs and introduce casual social conversation while the lows sit back and wait to be spoken to.

In keeping with the above results, it seems that people segregate themselves from classes much above their own. A recent survey found that 83 percent of newly married couples selected mates from their own or the next social class. Marriage between the butler and the millionare's daughter is rare. Social contact between a buyer and a division manager is likely to be just as rare. Perhaps this is related to a finding that indicates that low-status people feel ill at ease with those above them because they feel that they have relatively little to offer.

In that light, some sociologists have called status an exchange process. The theory is that people trade status just as they trade goods. When a high person talks to a low, he confers status in exchange for some benefit of a real or psychological nature. A negotiation takes place between them.

Status affects performance and perception as well as communication. People expect more from those of high rank and are rewarded, for those above tend to accept the obligation to perform. One study showed that the lows expected the highs to participate in community affairs. When highs were asked why they were involved, many replied that they were only doing what was expected of them. In another experiment, subjects were asked to estimate the future performance of high- and low-status individuals in tasks *unrelated* to their reputations. The finding was that those with high status were expected to do better. This led one researcher to conclude that "status breeds status."

People seem to have a need for confirming status in others. When they look at a low-ranking person they perceive him to be conforming, unsure and easily influenced. The man of position is seen as independent, self-motivated and assertive.

Although the evidence is by no means complete, the high-status man appears to have much more going for him in a negotiation than his low-ranking counterpart.

CONCLUSION

The question of status in negotiation is controversial. At my seminars, old hands sometimes express doubt about its importance. Their arguments are persuasive, for they insist that other factors—such as power—are more critical. I would be the first to agree that status in itself is not likely to win a negotiation. However, I believe that it plays an often neglected part in determining the outcome. Status has an effect on team leadership, decision-making, aspiration level and the perceptions of an opponent. Status is like money in the bank—it can be exchanged for something else of value.

CHAPTER 9

THE
ROLE OF
ROLE

ALL THE WORLD'S A STAGE,
AND ALL THE MEN AND WOMEN MERELY PLAYERS.

THEY HAVE THEIR EXITS AND THEIR ENTRANCES;
AND ONE MAN IN HIS TIME PLAYS MANY PARTS . . .

Shakespeare

SOW A THOUGHT, AND YOU REAP AN ACT.
SOW AN ACT, AND YOU REAP A HABIT.
SOW A HABIT, AND YOU REAP A CHARACTER.
SOW A CHARACTER, AND YOU REAP A DESTINY.

Charles Reade

About five years ago our team participated in a negotiation in Belleville, New Jersey, 3,000 miles from home. Belleville is a nice city, but hardly the place to spend a four-day Fourth of July weekend. To the relief of both parties a complicated agreement was concluded late July 3 and the weekend saved. I suspect that a disproportionate number of settlements are reached on the day before Christmas, New Year's and Thanksgiving.

A negotiator is a man torn on every side by roles imposed on him. In this chapter we will try to develop an understanding of conflicting roles in relation to negotiation. The concept of role originates in the theater. Roles, like parts in a play, are patterns of behavior that are learned and interpreted. Actors perform different parts from play to play; each being a blend of the author's words and the actor's personality. Movie directors, with all their skill, make casting errors. Critics have commented that William Holden, so right for his part in "Stalag 17," has not been well cast since. Others thought Cary Grant was too old to play the lover in "Father Goose," and Liz Taylor too housewife-ish to be credible as Cleopatra. Executives, when selecting negotiators, sometimes fail to cast them well.

The *Bargaining Model of Role,* shown in Figure 5, is a way of looking at negotiation from the standpoint of the spokesman and those who affect his life. We know that a man does not always behave as expected. The model will help us to find out why. It will also help us to understand such concepts as role-sending, role-expectation, and role-receiving. The working of the model should become clear as we discuss each factor and weave them together.

ROLE-SENDERS AND ROLE-CONFLICT

Each of us belongs to many groups either on a formal or informal basis. We have ties to other men along political, religious, recreational and commercial lines. We play a part in each group and thereby accept certain duties in exchange for benefits. Among my role-senders, for example, are my wife, my boss, the tax-collector and my friend Bill.

The model shows that a negotiator has eight role-senders. Each evaluates his role differently and expects something else of him. In one way or another they tell him how they wish

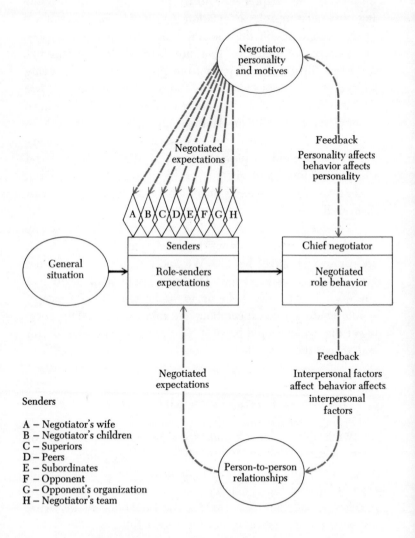

Senders

A – Negotiator's wife
B – Negotiator's children
C – Superiors
D – Peers
E – Subordinates
F – Opponent
G – Opponent's organization
H – Negotiator's team

Figure 5. BARGAINING MODEL OF ROLE

him to behave. This is rarely better illustrated than in a per-sonal-injury case where those with an equity in the final settle-ment include the person injured, the insurance company, the negligent party, the home-office claims executives, the local claims manager, the field claimsman and the independent ad-juster. Each plays a part in the behavior of the opposing attorneys. When so many people have expectations and send different role assumptions governing the behavior of one man, it is inevitable that role-conflict occurs.

The most common type of conflict occurs when two senders want different things. If my boss wants me to negotiate on Saturday, I cannot take my children to the football game. If I must be in Belleville, I cannot supervise my employees in Los Angeles. If an engineer must solve a technical problem on the assembly line, he cannot provide proper support at the conference table.

Occasionally conflict is created when one party sends two roles that are incompatible. For example, it is not uncommon for engineering to demand that a buyer negotiate a low price but at the same time provide him no latitude or time to solicit competitive bids. A buyer's wife may want him to earn more money but insist that he be home for dinner promptly at five. Another source of conflict occurs when the demands of a role are incompatible with a man's personal values. An acquaintance of mine is an executive in the trucking business. It's a dirty business, with lots of side payments, including bribes and callgirls. He hates that part of the job but knows no other way to make a good living.

Role-conflict creates ambiguity and tension. A negotiator cannot play every part assigned him but must instead negotiate an acceptable performance with those who have an equity in his behavior. He must comply with some demands, modify others and even ignore a few. How he resolves conflict depends upon his personality and relationship to the various role-senders.

HOW PERFORMANCE ALTERS ROLE EXPECTATIONS

When a wife expects her husband home from work at five but he keeps coming home at ten, she soon learns to expect him late. She may even decide after a while that he is a pretty good guy for coming home at eight. Harry S Truman accepted the role of President with surprising vigor while Dwight D. Eisenhower did not. Each shaped the assignment to his own personality and philosophy. In the same way the behavior of a negotiator changes the expectations of those he serves.

The best way to look at the relationship between a role-sender and role-receiver is to imagine them negotiating with each other. The sender says, "This is what I want you to do." The receiver replies, "Be reasonable, you're not the only one who wants something of me." Both soon realize that they must compromise or break up the relationship. Where they settle will depend, as in any other negotiation, upon the personality, needs, relationships and bargaining strengths of the parties. The problem is further complicated by the fact that seven other powerful role-senders are simultaneously trying to have their demands heard. Nobody succeeds in getting everything he wants.

People learn to accept the level of role-performance they get. Once a role-player achieves a higher performance level, others learn to expect the same. Conversely, we adjust to those who fail to live up to our expectations. There is a constant feedback between role-performance and role-expectation.

PERSONALITY AND ROLE

The amount of research in this field is not great, but a few observations are warranted. One investigator discovered that open-minded people like to take on new roles while authoritarians tend to reject them. In another study it was found that people differ in sensitivity to role-conflict. Those most affected tend to be introverted, emotional and intensely motivated to a particular goal.

There is experimental as well as observational evidence that behavior in a role can affect personality. People in a role seem to say, "I am, therefore I must be." In those cases where behavior is incompatible with role requirements the role-player suffers a loss of identity and becomes anxious.

We still know too little about the relationship of role and personality. Social psychologists Daniel Katz and Robert L. Kahn have contributed to our understanding by their writing and experimentation.[19] There is, however, little doubt that the role of negotiator is one of great conflict. It is he who must reconcile the rigorous demands of others in an acceptable long-lasting fashion. It appears that this can best be accomplished by a man who is mature, open-minded, outgoing and self-controlled.

CONCLUSION

In the first chapter we described the Starmatic transaction. Had the owner of the company been sensitive to the importance of role he would never have permitted his people to bargain without at least relieving them of some day-to-day responsibilities. Role contributes to the balance of power. A systematic analysis of it will permit a negotiator to understand the human forces that contribute to his opponent's perception of risk and uncertainty. If you want to know what makes your opponent "run," take a good look at the people he runs for.

CHAPTER 10

NEEDS,
GOALS
AND ACTION

TO THE MILLIONS WHO HAVE TO GO WITHOUT TWO MEALS
A DAY THE ONLY ACCEPTABLE FORM IN WHICH GOD DARE
APPEAR IS FOOD.

Gandhi

MAN DOTH NOT LIVE BY BREAD ALONE.

Deuteronomy

Over 2,000 years ago Aristotle observed, "Pleasure and no-
bility between them supply the motives of all action what-
soever." In Washington, our government is trying an experiment
in motivation. They have awarded college scholarships to a
group of poor eleven-year-olds of average ability and will continue to do so for a number of years. The government wants
to find out whether they will work harder in school if assured
of a free college education. This, you will agree, is quite an
extension of Aristotle's simple premise.

Every business transaction involves an exchange of motives. In order to understand motivation from a bargaining standpoint, we will do three things: 1) build a basic framework by which needs and goals can be recognized, 2) develop a model that integrates needs, goals and perception and 3) propose a systematic method by which goal satisfaction may be increased for both parties.

THE BASIC NEEDS

Human behavior is motivated by a desire to gain satisfaction. One useful and intuitively appealing way to understand behavior was developed by Abraham H. Maslow,[20] who says that men organize their needs by ranking them from most to least important. Since it is never possible to satisfy all needs, those most pressing get in line first. One can imagine these wants as a five-story pyramid. The structure shown in Figure 6 includes: 1) basic survival, 2) safety, 3) love, 4) worth and 5) self-actualization. It is popularly called *Maslow's Hierarchy of Needs*.

Those needs at the base are the strongest. A hungry man will search for food and let his desire for love or worth wait. The men in Andersonville Prison during the Civil War became cannibals when driven by extreme hunger. At the top of the pyramid man is seen doing what he can do best: realizing his highest potential. Sammy Davis, Jr., catches the flavor of this idea when he sings "I've Gotta Be Me." Poor people spend most of their energy satisfying lower-level wants while those well off are more concerned with "being me." Although man does not live by bread alone, there are only a few people on earth deeply concerned with self-actualization. Most have to work too hard to live from day to day.

Men have needs on all five levels regardless of their circumstances. When lower-level needs are reasonably satisfied, energy is then directed toward higher needs. As one is filled another takes its place in an endless chain, as needs and aspirations change throughout a man's life.

Needs are related to goals. When a need is unsatisfied, behavior is energized toward a goal. In that sense needs energize behavior while goals give direction to it. A goal such as money is capable of satisfying many needs at once. Let us look at the goals of man for a deeper insight into why men negotiate.

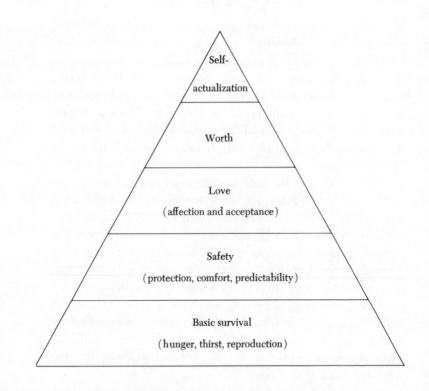

Figure 6. MASLOW'S HIERARCHY OF NEEDS

GOALS

A man may satisfy his need for worth by being a good father or running General Motors. This is not far-fetched. During the 1968 election a reporter commented that Richard Nixon appeared more sure of himself than he had earlier. He attributed some of this gain in self-confidence to the fact that the candidate had raised two lovely and vivacious daughters. Like most fathers, I know that this is not an easy thing to do.

Hunger may be satisfied by eating bread, wild pheasant or chocolate-covered grasshoppers in a Beverly Hills delicatessen. Self-actualization may consist of writing a book or seeking great wealth. Men strive to achieve objectives in order to satisfy unfilled needs. A brief look at nine of man's major goals will be helpful.

Money. Many believe that in Western society money is the most important goal. To suggest that other goals may be just as potent appears on the surface to defy common sense. William F. Whyte, in his study on the motivational impact of money, found that workers indeed wanted to increase their incomes. However, they were unwilling to do so at the expense of losing control over their work environment.[21] David C. McClelland, in another study, discovered that people with a high need for achievement had a relatively low regard for money. They looked at it as a symbol or measure of achievement rather than as a value in itself.[7] Frederick Herzberg confirmed that money was not a real motivator but rather what he called "hygienic" in nature. Men did not wish to fall behind in the money race, but they were not inclined to raise productivity for the sake of a higher income.[22]

The evidence indicates that money is only one of many goals men strive for. It will remain important in capitalistic societies for a long time. However, we may predict that its relative position among men's goals will decline as society becomes more affluent.

Power and Competence. These twin goals are related. Both reflect the need of men to control their destinies. In some persons the goal is mastery over tasks, in others mastery over people. We strive for independence from an early age and continue to value it throughout life.

Knowledge. Men have a universal desire to know and understand the world around them. An Australian bushman wants to know why the chief is always angry or how best to make a simple tool. Civilized man, having learned that knowledge is the road to power and income, spends a large part of his resources in pursuit of this goal.

Achievement. Some men work hard because they wish to do something worthwhile for its own sake. They have a need to achieve, which is more important than the rewards involved. (Achievement and its relationship to negotiation was discussed in Chapter 4.)

Excitement and Curiosity. All men share a desire for excitement and stimulation, but not in the same way. I know men who love to negotiate no matter what is at stake because they find it exciting. I met a wealthy German businessman in Mexico who enjoyed bargaining with the natives rather than touring museums and churches. He was prepared to bargain for the most inconsequential of trinkets and was willing to deadlock for as little as a half-peso (4¢).

The twin goals of excitement and curiosity play a part at every need level. Hungry as they are, people grow tired of the same diet. In my opinion, much of extramarital sex can be explained on the basis of simple curiosity—so too the lure of Las Vegas gambling tables.

Social. People need people. Americans in particular seem to have a greater need than others to join organizations. Management theorists have long urged executives to pay attention to the informal organization, for they believe that the key to increased productivity lies in motivating this small, unofficial social group.

Social goals are valued by corporations as well as individuals. The social value of a merger with IBM exceeds that of a merger with Automatic Sprinkler.

Recognition and Status. People want to stand out. The status symbol of an executive suite is cherished by those who enjoy its benefits. Office size, bathroom keys, executive typewriters and job titles are marks of distinction. One California conglomerate recognized the importance of job title early in its corporate life and gave the title of vice-president to men doing work that in other firms merely rated the title of manager. It made their recruiting problems easier. Men are attracted to objectives that enhance their ability to stand out among others.

Security and Risk-Avoidance. The fact that the future is unknown forces men to be concerned with reducing its dangers. A buyer can no more afford to risk his job on an unknown supplier than a business firm can afford to chance a large loss on a sale. The insurance industry has grown rapidly in response to the security goal inherent in all of us.

In personal-injury cases the element of uncertainty plays a large part in the balance of power and the ultimate settlement. Some attorneys are capable of living with uncertainty while others collapse under this pressure.

Congruence. I once saw a hardened old moneylender say to a borrower who was behind in his payments, "If you're so smart, why ain't you rich?" The remark demoralized the borrower because it undermined his congruence goal. The borrower thought of himself as being smart and disliked being confronted with the fact that he was nearly bankrupt.

People search for balance in their lives. Men who have power or knowledge find poor earnings insufferable. They behave in such a way as to remove the source of imbalance.

The nine goals, money, power, knowledge, achievement, excitement, social, recognition, security and congruence, are what people negotiate for. Perception of goals plays an important part in the process of gaining satisfaction and reaching agreement.

PERCEPTION

An opponent does not usually tell you what his goals are. To find out you have to do a great deal of homework. The model shown as Figure 7, *Goals, Needs and Perception*, provides a useful framework for analyzing an opponent's goals in a thoughtful, disciplined way.

A glance at the model will show that six perceptual questions are suggested. The first three deal with the negotiator's goals while the last three are concerned with the opponent's.

I. Questions related to Negotiator's goals:
   a. How does Negotiator perceive his own goals?
   b. How does Negotiator believe that Opponent perceives Negotiator's goals?
   c. How does Negotiator want Opponent to perceive Negotiator's goals?

II. Questions related to Opponent's goals:
   d. How does Negotiator perceive Opponent's goals?
   e. How does Opponent perceive his own goals?
   f. How does Opponent want Negotiator to perceive Opponent's goals?

The mere asking of a question does not guarantee an answer. Assumptions based on facts and observations must be made. One thing that makes the job a bit easier is that people are predictable.

PEOPLE ARE PREDICTABLE

Only rarely do we read of a person who acts in an un-predictable way, and it makes for interesting copy when we do. For every Paul Gauguin who goes to the South Pacific to "do his thing" a million businessmen trudge to the offices each

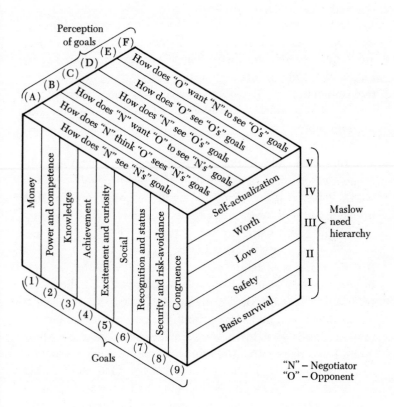

Figure 7. GOALS, NEEDS AND PERCEPTION

day. Now and then we are silently sympathetic to the trusted bank employee who embezzles thousands and runs to the gambling casinos for one big splurge. But for most of us there is a very good chance we will do tomorrow what we did yesterday.

The best way to predict behavior is to look at a person's history. A careful study of an opponent's habits, temperament, opinions and values will reveal useful patterns. The personality traits of a man tend to guide his behavior in accordance with the individual's major intentions.

People react to frustration and stress in recognizable patterns. Some behave with patience, humor and creativity. Others are defensive and unrealistic. They make excuses, bury facts, forget, blame others, become hostile, withdraw or become emotional under stress. If we know what they did yesterday, we can make a sounder assumption about the defense they will use tomorrow.

Values do not change from day to day. A man who has a history of double-dealing can be expected to use the technique once more. A penny-pincher will pinch pennies. A man with a reputation for taking risks will be predisposed in that direction in the future. An opponent who places great value on status will go on searching for status.

When looking at past behavior it is well to keep in mind that a person will act in accordance with what he believes to be his own self-interest. We can assume that he believes his behavior to be rational and wishes to protect his self-image. As outsiders, you and I may think the person wrong, but we must recognize that his behavior makes sense from his viewpoint. I was once responsible for disposing of company equipment and requested offers from dealers. One made what appeared to be a ridiculously high offer, so high it looked like a mistake. Afterward I learned that he was the only man thoroughly familiar with the old equipment. For a few dollars he was able to repair and resell a very expensive piece of

electronic gear. When predicting behavior from past performance it is safe to assume that an opponent is "crazy like a
fox." He acts in his own best interest.

Everything a man does serves to protect or enlarge his
self-image. Self-image roots go back to childhood experiences.
One can safely assume that an opponent will follow patterns
that previously proved successful from his viewpoint. Perhaps
the best way to learn about an opponent is to follow the advice
of the psychiatrist; ask questions, listen, speak rarely, observe
and be nonjudgmental. If you have the patience to listen, the
opponent's self-image will emerge.

We should remember that all predictions are guesses. The
more information we have the better we can guess. Sir Francis
Bacon advised, "All practice is to discover, or to work. Men
discover themselves in trust, in passion, at unawares and of
necessity, when they would have something done and cannot
find apt pretext."[17]

MAXIMIZING GOAL SATISFACTION

People transact business for the purpose of gaining goal
satisfaction. It is possible for a negotiator to increase the satisfaction of both parties through a disciplined approach toward
problem-solving. This can best be done by asking four questions during the problem-solving process:

1. *How can both benefit by Negotiator working for the
achievement of joint goals?* This, for example, may be accomplished when a Negotiator (buyer) provides a seller with
specialized technical personnel in order to assure good seller
performance.

2. *How can both benefit by Negotiator working actively
for achievement of Opponent's goals?* This can be illustrated
by a situation in which the Opponent (seller) is rewarded with

favorable trade-journal publicity. The seller's recognition and status goals are satisfied by publicizing his association with an important national-defense program or customer.

3. *How can both benefit by Negotiator helping Opponent to work for Opponent's goals?* For example, a Negotiator (seller) may offer to provide the buyer's organization with access to computer facilities or technical literature otherwise unavailable. In that way the buyer is in a better position to satisfy his own money and knowledge goals.

4. *How can both parties benefit by Negotiator giving up some individual or joint goals in favor of others?* This situation arises when a prime contractor and subcontractor agree to *accept and share* joint risks in order to get a big contract from the government. In this case risk-avoidance goals have been sacrificed in favor of future money and power goals.

No group of questions can automatically guarantee that two parties will take the right action to maximize goal satisfaction. It takes creative search, good will and patience as well. The suggested questions are only a step in the right direction.

THE EXCHANGE VALUE OF MOTIVES

We negotiators are always faced with a conflict of interest. Rarely if ever do the priorities and values of the corporation mesh precisely with our own. Sometimes a reduction of $100 from the seller's asking price can be important to the buyer but almost meaningless to his company. The buyer may desperately need the reduction to prove to his boss that the opponent was tough but not impregnable.

Personal values are not corporate values. It may be advantageous from a company viewpoint to use a deadlock maneuver, but it may involve so much personal risk to the negotiator that he dare not use it. Can one equate the potential loss of a million dollars to the company against the need for job security? No. All we can do is differentiate between corporate and individual priorities. If we do our job well, it is likely that we will achieve our objectives while assuring that the total exchange of needs, goals and goods permits both parties to enjoy greater satisfaction.

CHAPTER 11

THE
ANATOMY OF
NEGOTIATION

BUT BEFORE THESE THINGS WERE SEPARATED, WHEN ALL
THINGS WERE TOGETHER, NOT EVEN WAS ANY COLOR
CLEAR AND DISTINCT; FOR THE MIXTURE OF ALL THINGS
PREVENTED IT, THE MIXTURE OF MOIST AND DRY, OF THE
WARM AND COLD, AND OF THE BRIGHT AND THE DARK; FOR
NONE OF THE OTHER THINGS AT ALL RESEMBLES THE ONE
THE OTHER.

Anaxagoras

Irving Stone, in *The Agony and the Ecstasy*, describes
Michelangelo's drive to understand human anatomy as follows:
"A sculptor could not create movement without perceiving
what caused the propulsion; could not portray tension, conflict,
drama, strain, force unless he saw every fiber at work within
the body. . . . Learn anatomy he must!" To understand negotiation we must understand its anatomy. Our task therefore is
to do what Michelangelo did, dissect this thing called negotiation into two main sections, content (or substance) and time.
I think you will agree that after the operation the patient will
never look the same.

In exchanges between persons or nations, five levels of bargaining take place: 1) a *share*-bargaining process, 2) a *problem-solving* process, 3) an *attitudinal*-bargaining process, 4) a *personal*-bargaining process and 5) an *in-group*-bargaining process. Four of these processes are discussed at length in the excellent book *A Behavioral Theory of Labor Negotiations* by Richard E. Walton and Robert B. McKersie.[23] We will look at each process briefly and then direct attention to the anatomy of time.

THE SHARE-BARGAINING PROCESS

Buying a used car from a private party is a good example of *share* bargaining. If the seller's minimum price is $1,000 and the buyer's maximum is $1,300, then any agreement between these points will be better than no deal for both. When a settlement is reached at $1,200 the seller has gained a larger share of the range than the buyer. In share bargaining, what one party gains the other loses. When most of us speak of negotiation it is this *rationing* process that we normally think about.

Share bargaining is concerned with issues involving the *division* of money, property, power or status. For example, price is almost always an issue whether it involves the initial contract, incentive formulas or an adjustment for specification changes. In aerospace negotiations, patent rights and warranty obligations are often serious bargaining issues, for they can "make or break" a company, depending on how they are settled. Issues always involve important conflicts of interest between parties.

I recently attended a conference in which a medical doctor was asked to make an educational film for a producer. The major issue was not money. Instead it was the doctor's right to scrap the film if it did not suit his professional image. This

issue was so important to both parties that it was never resolved.

Share bargaining involves a high degree of self-centered-
ness. If a party is to achieve high targets he must discover all
he can about the opponent while hiding information about
himself. Successful share bargaining involves intensive fact-
finding, analysis, secrecy and tact. For instance, at a negotiation several months ago an engineer innocently told a supplier
that his proposal was the only one of six approved from a
technical standpoint. In the engineer's zeal to work out specifications the company bargaining position was weakened. When
confronted with the results of his disclosure, the engineer explained that the seller probably knew as much about the
competitive situation as we did. It was a foolish and costly
assumption.

The goal of share bargaining is to find a settlement point
that resolves the conflict of interest in one's own favor. In that
light it makes little sense to say or do anything that might
conceivably improve the bargaining position of the opponent.

THE PROBLEM-SOLVING PROCESS

In *every* negotiation it is possible for both parties to help
each other at no expense to themselves. If each understands
the problems of the other and openly tries to solve these problems together, both can benefit. We call this the *problem-solving* process. Let me illustrate with a practical example.

I know a man who collects credit cards but never uses
them for borrowing. Unlike most of us he *earns* money from
his cards. When shopping for a washing machine he visits
several discount houses, compares model prices and buys from
the store quoting the lowest price. As the manager writes up
the credit charge the man suggests that he be given a discount
for cash. It works almost every time. A majority of store man-

agers would rather get cash than incur paperwork and delay. They prefer to grant a 5 percent discount to a customer than pay 5 percent to a finance company. He has discovered a basic principle of the problem-solving process—that is, to gain satisfaction for one or both parties at no expense to either.

Opportunities to solve mutual problems between buyer and seller exist in *every* contracting situation. When an engineer and supplier work together to define specifications they are engaged in problem-solving bargaining. Other examples of problem-solving concern matters such as progress payments, system approvals and billing methods. It is not unusual for a buyer to issue a proposal request with an excess of standard and special clauses to protect his legal position. However, these terms may conflict with a supplier's business procedures and create unnecessary hardship. For example, if a seller's accounting system is on a monthly basis it may be expensive to provide cost reports weekly. In that case both parties may gain if they settle for a midmonth estimate and an accurate report monthly. The same potential for joint gain exists in other parts of the contract.

The policy of purchasing supplies from the lowest of several bidders is a sound practice *that can be improved* simply by recognizing the problem-solving process. Supplies should be purchased from the lowest of several bidders *after* opportunities for joint problem-solving have been considered with one or more of the lower bidders. A seller may be willing to grant options, stock-reserve quantities or provide favorable credit terms in a manner not covered by his proposal. In any case, gainful arrangements can be made for both parties. It makes no sense to close one's mind to the gains available from joint problem-solving merely because three bids have been received.

All that is necessary for success in problem-solving is adequate time, good will, open-mindedness and motivation. A supportive, nonjudgmental, communicative climate can help both parties find new ways to assist each other. Successful problem-solvers reveal rather than conceal; they show empathy rather than exploit. When such a climate prevails the potential for mutual gain will be large.

ATTITUDINAL BARGAINING

What is the best way of containing an aggressive opponent? Is it best to respond in a militant, pacifist or mixed fashion? Research indicates that an aggressive opponent is best contained by a mixed strategy—that is, a strategy that is sometimes cooperative and sometimes aggressive, but is not patterned in a predictable fashion. Unfortunately, when one party is conciliatory and the other cantankerous, the imbalance usually favors the competitive player in the short run.[24] It is therefore necessary to engage in attitudinal bargaining in order to assure that negotiations are conducted in a climate that results in stable final agreements.

Relationships and attitudes between opponents are negotiable. The parties invariably start with preconceptions about the best way to act toward each other. The basis for these preconceptions have deep roots. As a person matures, his way of looking at the world and his feelings about it result in a relatively stable pattern of behavior. Beliefs, opinions and biases tend to be consistent with attitudes. Because attitudes are both emotional and rational they are hard to change. Nevertheless, a satisfactory negotiation cannot take place until both parties are willing to modify their attitudes sufficiently to engage in share and problem-solving processes.

All of us are familiar with the breakdown of bargaining at the international level. The Red Chinese have nourished a long-smoldering hatred of America and thereby made it difficult to transact even a minimum of essential diplomatic business. Negotiations between Arab and Jew are at an impasse for similar reasons. Conversely, American attitudes toward the Canadians and Australians are such that business runs smoothly no matter how difficult the issue.

I have seen commercial negotiations falter for emotional reasons. Ten years ago a competent Negro contract manager was required to negotiate with an Alabama manufacturer. The black man was treated shabbily from the start, as there were no decent hotels that would accommodate him. Of course, the white team members volunteered to join him in the Negro district of town but soon learned that black townspeople did not welcome confrontations of this sort. So the negotiation never got off the ground. The buyer's company should have foreseen the problem instead of exposing everybody to an impossible situation. In a similar vein, negotiations break down when men have strong feelings toward an opponent's race, religion or political preference. Such men should step aside and let someone else do the job. It is hard enough to understand the facts without introducing the distortion that comes from emotional hangups.

Buyers and sellers must understand their biases if they want to be effective. Buyers are sometimes excessively distrustful and domineering with sales representatives. Salesmen, all too often, have a tendency to view buyers as clerical bureaucrats and hagglers looking for a free bottle at Christmas time. Many government contracting officers view the defense supplier as an exploiter whose only interest is windfall profits. These viewpoints are more often than not indefensible. Although attitudes are by their nature emotional, an awareness of one's disposition can lead to some degree of objectivity.

The attitudinal-bargaining process assumes that desired relationships can be structured through negotiation with an opponent. Five relationships are basic to most bargaining situations. They are: 1) extreme aggression, 2) mild aggression for deterrent purposes, 3) mutual accommodation, 4) open cooperation and 5) direct collusion with the opponent. In conducting business it is necessary to decide which of these five relationships is appropriate from a strategic standpoint. For example, we may decide that American long-range goals with respect to mainland China are best served by a policy of mutual accommodation. Considering the extremely aggressive attitude of the Red Chinese it may be necessary to pursue a policy of mild aggression modified by occasional acts of hostility, accommodation and open cooperation. This mixed strategy may serve to communicate our determination to reach a mutual-accommodation relationship. Attitudinal bargaining plays a part in every negotiation.

THE PERSONAL-BARGAINING PROCESS

When two men sit on opposite sides of the table each is confronted by an additional adversary: himself. You will recall the negotiation that took place in Belleville on July 3. From a personal standpoint there was one hidden issue: to return to Los Angeles prior to the four-day holiday.

An individual struggles to reconcile competing needs and goals by negotiating a suitable arrangement with the outside world. An exchange process goes on within him in which one need is traded for another. In the last analysis he chooses a pattern of behavior that he believes will provide the most satisfaction for the energy involved.

It is evident that a negotiator *must strike a bargain with himself*. The outcome of a negotiation may well depend upon how one party or the other reconciles role-conflict.

THE IN-GROUP-BARGAINING PROCESS

Invariably negotiators bargain for others as well as themselves. A man may transact business with a real-estate broker while away from his family, but they are as involved as though they were at the table. It is important to understand how a man bargains with those he represents—that is, the people in his *own* organization or social group.

In a strict sense, organizations do not have objectives, but people within them do. Each member of a decision-making coalition has his own level of aspirations and a *personal definition* of the critical issues. The negotiator is but one member of the coalition that establishes group goals. Furthermore, each of the participants has an individual value system and represents a different degree of power, status and bargaining skill. What we normally call bargaining objectives is really an outcome of the *in-group* process.

Conflict within an organization is the result of differences in facts, goals, methods or values among members. The variations cause group members to look at issues in a personal way and to search for group solutions that provide as much safety and satisfaction as possible to themselves. In such cases, the negotiator is faced with the uncomfortable task of reconciling a bewildering number of in-group demands. Unfortunately, the opponent is not inclined to be helpful.

The negotiator's dilemma may be intense. If, as a member of the coalition, he is passive about participating in its deliberations, he may encounter a difficult situation at the table. On the other hand, if he decides to actively influence the coalition members into lowering their aspirations, he may be accused of not believing in the cause. The negotiator's boundary role between his organization and that of the opponent requires good judgment in dealing with both factions.

There are buyers who resolve the dilemma in the worst possible way. They concentrate on reducing the aspiration level of their own coalition instead of the opponent's. As a result they rarely fail to meet a target, for their wants are low from the start. These buyers usually have trouble when they have a limited budget or a tough-minded boss.

How a negotiator copes with stress caused by in-group demands is critical. He may respond in either an active or passive fashion, depending upon his personality and perception of the situation. An active response will consist of efforts to suspend final group judgment on expectations until maximum information is available. The active negotiator will also cope with unrealistic goals by persuading members to modify aspirations on the basis of new inputs from the bargaining table.

A passive advocate may take an entirely different approach. He may permit a deadlock to develop and let the members figure their own way out. A clever man can rationalize discrepancies between actual and expected performance after making a half-hearted attempt to achieve goals. Passive advocates have also been known to quietly advise opponents that their own organization is not to be taken seriously about certain demands. It is obvious that whenever possible active negotiators should be selected. Furthermore, they should be granted sufficient prestige and personal security to assure that they speak their minds without fear.

An appreciation of the in-group-bargaining process permits a negotiator to understand how an opponent makes strategic and tactical decisions. With this knowledge he may adjust his own plans to change the opponent's in-group values and expectations.

It is not possible to do justice to the five bargaining processes in a short chapter. A detailed discussion of four of these processes is available in the book *A Behavioral Theory of Labor Negotiation*.

NEGOTIATION — A THREE-ACT DRAMA

Soon after President Nixon took office he visited Europe. Upon returning he was questioned by reporters about the status of Vietnam negotiations, which had produced no results for three months. The President stated that talks were entering

Phase II, the hard-bargaining stage. Where did this phrase come from, and what did he mean? For an answer we may look at the research of Ann Douglas, who spent ten years of her life in a box seat at the labor-negotiation table.[25]

Ann Douglas not only attended innumerable bargaining sessions but was privileged to interview the parties during and after each day's events and gathered information that is ordinarily confidential. She concluded that negotiations followed the pattern of a three-act play. Phase I was "oratorical fireworks." In this act both parties behaved in an aggressive fashion, but when interviewed they maintained a warm personal regard for each other. Both realized that what was being said was directed to those back home rather than to each other.

The President correctly described the next phase in his interview, for it is in Phase II that hard bargaining takes place and the adversaries become serious, patrolling the settlement range searching for areas of compromise. Retreat from sham positions is slow but measured, and each listens for subtle signs of concession. Behavior becomes uncertain as the parties introduce confusion by deliberately generating misunderstanding, delay and resistance into the process. Nothing is taken for granted. Each party tests the intent of the other on issue after issue.

Phase III starts with a strong search for *realistic* resistance points and is marked by crises and settlement. *In-group bargaining* plays a critical part as negotiators establish close communication links to important members of their organization. At the same time the negotiators experience greater freedom from less significant members of the coalition not in attendance. The atmosphere becomes tense and uncertain. During this late phase the negotiators find themselves in a strange new relationship—that is, as a "negotiator-opponent" combination *united* against unreasonable pressures of the outside nonconference world.

		Steps	Function
Preconference negotiation stage		1	Req't formulation
		2	Formal procurement phase
		3	Formal negotiation conference planning, organization, fact-finding, and analysis
Conference negotiation stage	Phase I (verbal fireworks)	1	Introduct. Rules and tentative agenda agreement
		2	Establish maximum negotiating range and identify problems and issues Revise plans
	Phase II (hard bargaining)	3	Establish settlement and conflict range Modify range Solve problems
		4	Conflict-range negotiation
	Phase III (crisis)	5	Closure and agreement
Postconference negotiation stage		1	Agreement elaboration (formal contract formulation)
		2	Approval coordination
		3	Administrative elaboration and integration (formal and informal)
		4	Agreement antithesis, resynthesis and closure

Figure 8. TIME-PHASED NEGOTIATION MODEL

Bargaining subprocess	Share	Problem-solving	Attitudinal	In-group	Personal
	Low	High	High	Low	Low
	Med	Med	High	High	Low
	Med	High	Med	High	Med
	Med	Med	High	Med	Med
	High	Med	Med	Med	Med
	High	Med	Med	Med	Med
	High	Med	Med	High	High
	High	Med	High	High	High
	Low	Med	High	High	Med
	Low	Low	Med	Med	Med
	Med	High	High	Med	Med
	High	High	High	High	High

As the Phase III deadline approaches, alternatives are presented in rapid fashion. Statements of a private and semiofficial nature become very important. Agreement is finally reached and recorded by memorandum, after which the parties invariably express mutual good will and respect. Both are glad to have it over with.

The next time you are in a negotiation, see if Ann Douglas' observations apply. I believe they will.

TIME-PHASED NEGOTIATION

My concept of the time dimension is compatible with the Douglas theory but stems from a somewhat different viewpoint. It perceives the negotiation process as a *continuum* rather than an *episode*. The *Time-Phased Negotiation Model* shown in Figure 8 incorporates the Douglas cycle in the conference stage of bargaining.

The three stages of bargaining include a preconference, conference and postconference time period. In the preconference stage, requirements are definitized, objectives formulated, procurement processes inaugurated and formal prenegotiation conference activities initiated. Such activities include negotiation-planning, organization, fact-finding and analysis. During the conference stage, five steps take place. In the first, parties negotiate an agenda and rules of order. In the next they attempt to establish settlement range and identify problems and issues. The third step is characterized by range modification and problem-solving followed by hard bargaining. Closure and agreement mark the last step of this stage. The postconference stage is critical because the negotiation process is imperfect and encourages conflict between *problem-solving and share bargaining*. This stage consists of four activities: agreement elaboration, agreement approval, contract administration and final contract closure.

CONCLUSION

A blending of time factors and bargaining subprocesses is shown in Figure 8. In considering appropriate strategy and tactics it is necessary to perceive the overall process along a broad time front where each subprocess changes in importance. For example, the model shows how the relative importance of share bargaining and problem-solving changes continuously during the overall cycle.

Anaxagoras observed, "Before these things were separated . . . not even was any color clear and distinct." Hopefully we have by our dissection made negotiation more clear than before. In any case, an awareness of the anatomy of time and bargaining processes cannot help but contribute to better results at the table.

CHAPTER 12

THE EXPECTED-
SATISFACTION
THEORY

WE CAN ONLY HOPE TO OBSERVE PHENOMENA SYSTE-
MATICALLY IF WE HAVE A SET OF INSTRUCTIONS THAT
TELL US WHAT TO LOOK FOR. THESE SETS SIMPLY ARE
DIFFERENT THEORIES; SOME WAYS OF LOOKING AT
"REALITY" ARE USEFUL, OTHERS ARE NOT.

Peter Newman

Most high-level executives are more theoretical than they profess to be. They generally hire men, make product decisions and enter new markets with an uncanny accuracy that can only be explained on the basis of sensible theories about people and economics. Good theory is likely to lead to good practice because it is a useful way of looking at reality.

Expected satisfaction is a theory that provides a framework by which the process can be better understood. The theory serves two purposes: 1) it permits negotiation to be seen in a dramatic new way, and 2) it helps shatter a number of long-held business beliefs.

THE EXPECTED-SATISFACTION THEORY

The *Satisfaction Model of Negotiation* is shown in Figure 9. The model applies to transactions between people as well as countries. It applies as well to buying a house as to buying a missile system. The best way to understand the theory is by

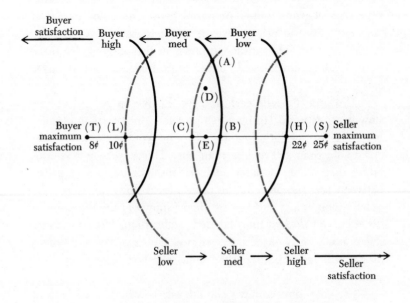

Proposal	Price	Average unit price, cents	Seller's[*] total profit, cents	Gain or loss of satisfaction, relative to proposal (A)	
				Buyer	Seller
(A)	1 for 15¢	15.0	5	—	—
(B)	3 for 45¢	15.0	15	None	Gain
(C)	5 for 55¢	11.0	5	Gain	None
(D)	2 for 28¢	14.0	8	Gain	Gain
(E)	5 for 63¢	12.6	13	Gain	Gain

[*] Seller's Cost = 10 cents

Figure 9. SATISFACTION MODEL
OF NEGOTIATION

example, after which we will state the theory in simple terms.

Imagine for a moment that a tourist is entering a small grocery store in a Mexican village where prices are not marked. On the shelf are five dusty cans of Campbell's beans. The tourist loves these beans and has been without them for a long time. He would not object to buying all five at the right price, but would settle for one. From a price standpoint, the tourist would be delighted to pay 8¢, the normal California supermarket price, but is prepared to pay as much as 22¢ if necessary. As the price moves from 8¢ to 22¢ the tourist becomes less and less satisfied (shown in the diagram by three curved *solid* lines labeled "buyer high, buyer med and buyer low").

The grocer needs cash and would like to get rid of this slow-moving item. He operates on the principle that nothing must ever be sold at a loss, therefore he would rather do without a sale than sell at less than 10¢. The storekeeper is confident that sooner or later all five cans will be sold at prices between 10¢ and 25¢. As the price moves down from 25¢ the seller becomes less and less satisfied (shown in the diagram by three curved *dashed* lines labeled "seller high, seller med and seller low"). Any price between 10¢ and 22¢, the settlement range, will leave both parties more satisfied than if no deal is made.

The first question we should ask is whether there is a point of *equal* satisfaction for both. The second is whether there exists a point at which they will gain *equal* marginal satisfaction from the deal. The answer to both questions is, *not necessarily*.

The facts are that the grocer and tourist have entirely different value systems. The tourist has $100 in his wallet but refuses to be "taken" in any deal; he would rather walk away than pay 25¢ for a can of beans. The grocer *needs cash and every penny is important*, but he would rather do without than sell for less than 10¢. Furthermore, neither the tourist nor the grocer values the quality of Campbell's beans in the same way. Needless to say, there is no way to measure whether they can get equal satisfaction from the exchange. All that can be said is they will both gain satisfaction if the final price is between 10¢ and 22¢.

With that in mind let us now pick up the conversation at the point where both are considering whether to close the deal at 15¢ (shown as Proposal [A] in the diagram). At this price the grocer enjoys a 5¢ profit. Is this the best settlement for both parties? No.

The four proposals shown below are superior to Proposal (A):

Proposal (B)–If the grocer were wise, he would offer to sell three cans for 45¢, at which his profit would be 15¢. The tourist's average price would remain at 15¢. *This proposal would represent an improvement for the seller at no loss to the tourist.*

Proposal (C)–The tourist might counter with an offer to buy all five cans for 55¢, which would provide a large improvement for himself and still leave the grocer with the original 5¢ profit of Proposal (A).

Proposal (D)–If the above offer were refused, the tourist could propose to buy two cans for 28¢. In this case *both parties would be better off* because the grocer's profit would rise to 8¢ and the buyer's average cost fall to 14¢.

Proposal (E)–Finally, they would be wise to conclude a deal at five cans for 63¢, where the grocer earns 13¢ and the tourist pays only 12.6¢ per can. *There is no better deal possible for both in relation to the first offer.*

Proposals (B), (C) and (D) represent *trading*, or problem-solving, proposals. In each case an improved solution for one or both parties was possible by combining the needs of both in a package deal. Finally, a point was reached where they could no longer improve the satisfaction of one without hurting the other. If, in the example above, the grocer were to refuse the best offer and insist on 64¢ for five cans, then the tourist's unit cost would rise to 12.8¢ while the grocer's profit rose to 14¢. The grocer would benefit at the tourist's expense. Proposal (E) is therefore considered to be a share-bargaining proposal.

One more important point should be illustrated. Neither the tourist nor the grocer knows how much satisfaction he will get from the agreement. Each has *expectations* about the future. The grocer may make the deal, then see a 30¢-per-can tourist walk in a moment later. The tourist may open the cans and find them spoiled. The element of *expected satisfaction* is an integral part of every transaction. People evaluate future events in a personal way and attach different dollar and psychological values to them. They often pay a great deal for privileges that are rarely, if ever, enjoyed. For example, I know a couple who spend $500 a month in boat and membership fees at an exclusive yacht club while using the facilities only two or three times a year. Future events show a perverse tendency to vary from expectations, but each individual has his own discount rate for tomorrow's satisfaction. The fact that some are wild optimists and others are dour pessimists is also a vital part of the negotiation process.

A SUMMARY OF THE THEORY

The Expected-Satisfaction Theory may be summarized in terms of seven basic propositions:

Proposition 1–Negotiation is not simply a good deal for both parties. While each must gain something, it is *improbable* that they will gain equally.

Proposition 2–No two value systems are likely to be the same. The grocer's concept of beans and money was not identical with the tourist's. Men have more or less the same needs *but achieve different degrees of satisfaction* from reaching goals.

Proposition 3–In *every* negotiation the potential exists for the parties to improve their *joint* satisfaction at no loss to either. The more intense the search for joint improvement, the more likely people will be to find superior solutions. This process of joint improvement is called *problem-solving* bargaining.

Proposition 4–In every negotiation there is a point reached at which the gains of one party are won at the loss of the other. This process of rationing is called *share* bargaining.

Proposition 5–All transactions are based upon *future expectations* of satisfaction. No two men are likely to estimate future satisfactions in the same way.

Proposition 6–In the last analysis it is not goods or money or services that people exchange in the process of negotiation but satisfaction. Material things represent only the more visible aspects of a transaction.

Proposition 7–A negotiator can only make assumptions about an opponent's satisfaction, expectations and goals. One important purpose of negotiation is to test these assumptions. The opponent's real intentions can only be discovered by a process of vigorous probing because he himself may be only dimly aware of them.

CONCLUSION

The expected-satisfaction theory has practical significance for those who wish to bargain more effectively. It applies as well to interpersonal relations as it does to business and diplomacy. Good theory and good practice are intimately related. The expected-satisfaction theory is a useful way of looking at reality.

PART III

A Program for Performance

INTRODUCTION. *This book was written to improve the performance of negotiators by providing them a deeper insight into the process. If improvement is to be made, good theory and practice must merge at the bargaining table.*

We found in our surveys that professional negotiators placed great value on planning and preparation. The credo "Do your homework" makes good sense at work and at school. The problem in negotiation is that the assignment is obscure. Doing one's homework means so many different things to different people that it becomes an empty phrase. There are no guidelines or minimum standards.

This state of affairs is intolerable where large sums of money are at stake. There should be a framework by which we can say, "I have done the planning job well. I have asked the questions that must be asked and answered those questions that could be answered economically."

Before we can plan we have to know more about what a good plan consists of. In the three-dimensional model of planning we will offer a new way to look at the process. If our aspiration is to optimize performance it is necessary to go one step beyond planning. We must organize more effectively. I am convinced that it is not difficult or expensive to organize to win if we set our sights accordingly. Part III is mostly about planning, strategy, tactics and organization. In it you will find a practical program for a better performance.

CHAPTER 13

STRATEGY

I ASKED HIM, "WHAT BUSINESS ARE YOU IN?" "THE BUSI-
NESS OF MAKING MONEY," HE SAID. "BUT WHAT DO YOU
DO?" "ANYTHING THAT PAYS A PROFIT," HE REMARKED.
I SHOOK MY HEAD AS I LEFT HIS YACHT. "THAT'S NO
STRATEGY."

Anonymous

THE SIMPLE PLAN,
THAT THEY SHOULD TAKE, WHO HAVE THE POWER,
AND THEY SHOULD KEEP WHO CAN.

Wordsworth

Years ago I ran into a little thing in the *New Yorker* that made
a distinction between strategic and tactical planning.

"Long-range goals:
1. Health—more leisure
2. Money
3. Write book (play?)—fame ////??

"Immediate:
1. Pick up pattern at Hilda's
2. Change faucets—call plumber (who?)
3. Try yoghurt? ?"

From the Diary of a Lady

Strategic planning is concerned with long-range goals and values. Tactical planning is concerned with maneuvers, techniques and calling the plumber. Good strategy can be offset by poor tactics; good tactics can make the best of poor strategy. The effective negotiator is at home with both.

The survey in Chapter 3 found that planning was ranked first by most people. It is probably the one thing that negotiators do least well. In this chapter we will take a professional look at negotiation planning. Our purpose is to develop a framework that will have relevance for buyers, sellers, lawyers and diplomats.

NEGOTIATION PLANNING—A THREE-DIMENSIONAL VIEW

Planning has three dimensions: strategic, administrative and tactical. Strategic planning is concerned with long-range business goals. Administrative planning involves getting men and information where they are needed so that the negotiation goes smoothly. Tactical planning simply seeks to get the best possible results at the bargaining table.

Table 3 shows that the major decisions associated with strategy involve basic product-and-market relationships. On the other hand, tactics provide the necessary "firing line" response to bargaining; they are means toward ends.

This chapter will be concerned exclusively with the most important of the planning phases, strategic planning. First we will analyze four aspects of strategy: 1) product-market goals, 2) fact-finding, 3) worth-analysis and 4) decision-making. Then we will see how a big company does its planning and will close the chapter with remarks addressed to the problems of buyers and sellers. Nothing will be said of administrative planning except to point out the obvious: that resources must be organized to get good results at the conference table. All too often this aspect of negotiation is left to the last minute.

PRODUCT-MARKET GOALS

Had the railroads decided at the turn of the century that they were in the transportation business rather than the busi-

	Strategic planning (policy)	Administrative planning	Tactical planning (operational)
…roblem	To select and negotiate with source or sources that optimize overall company competitive position and objectives	To organize people, power and informational resources and to optimize negotiation performance	To optimize realization of negotiation potential
…ature of …roblem	Decide which strategic goals are most important, how much is wanted and how best to achieve major objectives	Organization, acquisition and development of people, power and informational resources	Determination of subgoals, persuasive arguments and means appropriate to reaching strategic goals; testing intent of opponent
Key …cisions	• Product-market mix • Make or buy mix • Constraints—customer and environment • Decision-making structure • Competition philosophy • Basic goals—technical, price, delivery, management • Trade-offs • Risk-taking and risk-identification • Power relationships • Attitude relationships • Fact-finding methods • Proposal and information control (security) • Ethical values • Selection of chief negotiator • Worth-analysis	• Organization: Team support, and special assistance • Information: Fact-finding, channels, analysis, security and assumption testing • Resources: Personnel, tools, training, facilities, third parties	• Subgoals: Issues, problems, targets, assumption and intent testing • Techniques: Agenda, questions, affirmative statements, concessions, listening, commitments, moves, threats, promises, recess, delays, deadlock, nonverbal communications, focal points and standards • Inoculation • Maneuvers: Timing, inspection association, authority, amount, brotherhood, diversion

Table 3. NEGOTIATION PLANNING—A THREE-DIMENSIONAL VIEW

ness of moving men and material along tracks, they would be among the most powerful corporations in America today. This strategic decision lost them the opportunity to enter and dominate the automobile and airplane markets in their infancy. It was a poor choice of product-market goals rather than a tactical error. A negotiator may also overlook major goals in his concern with making a good deal.

The foremost problem for a negotiation strategist is to make sensible product-and-market decisions. Long before negotiation starts, a seller must ask whether the customer represents the market to which he wishes to sell. At the same time a buyer must determine whether the product offered fits into his product-market mix. It makes little sense for Ford buyers to shop for expensive radial tires on a small car like Maverick or for a poor man to drive a Continental. Product-market strategy is a question of corporate *self-identity*. It asks, "What business am I in and how does this transaction fit into the picture." If the purchase or sale does not fit in, it shouldn't be considered at all.

Product-market decisions for the buyer are specifically concerned with make or buy, end-product pricing, quality of product, competition, exploitation of power and long-run supplier relationships. For the seller the decisions are similar. Where the buyer decides to "make or buy" an item, the seller may make an equivalent "sale, franchise or license" decision. Obviously the time to worry about product-and-market policy is not at the conference table. There is no "right" price for the wrong product.

FACT-FINDING AND SECURITY

Fact-finding and security are primarily strategic rather than tactical problems. Although a negotiator can learn much about an opponent at the table, the bulk of his information should come long before. At the same time, the problem of protecting one's bargaining position must not begin at the negotiation but be part of a long-range security program that operates on a year-round basis. There is, in my opinion, no other sensible way to look at this critical business function.

Information about proposals, costs, budgets, competition, technical matters and motives must be concealed. I know of one company that has a policy of quarantining its men at a hotel during the final weeks of a large proposal effort, with families permitted to visit only on weekends. Such extreme precautions are reserved only for major projects. However, the firm is also extraordinarily careful about lesser submittals. They learned years ago that unsecured information becomes available to competition surprisingly fast. Fact-withholding and fact-finding are not matters to be taken lightly.

A leading Democrat from California once said, "Money is the mother's milk of politics." I would paraphrase his remark by saying, "Fact-finding is the mother's milk of negotiation."

The question is, "How far should a negotiator go to learn about the motives and intimate business workings of an opponent?" General Motors went too far a few years ago when it used private detectives indiscriminately. A business negotiation is not a war for national survival. Corruption, bribery and electronic bugging should never be condoned. However, we would be insane not to protect ourselves in every possible way against these evils. We who are in business cannot delude ourselves into believing that the ethical standards of our children and our society can be any higher than those of the business community.

How then can we learn about an opponent's needs and goals. The answer lies in careful research and homework. The opponent's business history should be studied. An analysis of previous negotiations, both successful and not, will provide useful clues. Financial data can be obtained at little cost through channels such as Dun and Bradstreet, newspaper files, company biographies, financial statements, inside stock reports and public records of legal judgments. Sometimes much can be learned by simply visiting with an opponent and asking questions. Another way to learn is to ask questions of people who have done business with the opponent. I'll never forget one reference who volunteered that a contractor did marvelous work, except when he was drunk.

In one large company, information on suppliers is kept in a data bank. Purchasing agents are assigned responsibility to become expert on the production, financial and executive structure of specific suppliers. A dossier is kept on every important supplier executive and includes personal as well as business matters. Performance and negotiation history are used in a dynamic way to build bargaining power. This company has found that intelligent, well-coordinated fact-finding is the cornerstone of forceful negotiation.

WORTH-ANALYSIS

The third factor of strategic planning is *worth-analysis.* To start with, worth-analysis differs from cost-analysis. The difference is best illustrated by an evaluation I recently performed for a friend who was asked by a movie studio to make a training film. The question was, "What is a day's work worth?"

My friend is a professional man who spends part of his time lecturing and teaching. There were several ways to go about the analysis. If the loss of a day's time in the office were used as a base, the filming was worth $400. If we were to consider it a lecture, its value would be $1,000. If his special talent in the particular role were to be used as a standard, then an additional $1,500 in acting and scriptwriting fees was appropriate.

When the problem was viewed from a production standpoint, it became apparent that the day's work was worth $27,-000. This was because four days' filming could be crowded into one. A final figure was computed based upon the increase in sales revenue attributable to the use of his famous name. In worth-analysis all economic as well as psychological factors are pertinent. In cost-analysis it is often the data least important which comes to the forefront.

Worth is the power to satisfy wants. Its value depends upon what is considered useful or desirable to a person in a particular situation. Cost is only one of many elements that may be considered in assigning worth. If a $100 part is required on an assembly line and a one-day delay costs $2,000, a buyer is justified in paying $2,000 for the part if he can save a single day. It would make no difference if the supplier's cost were 1¢ or $10,000.

In many industries, and particularly the aerospace industry, pricing people are in a rut. Like a needle on a scratched record, they are stuck on cost, cost, cost. In that way the pricers avoid dealing with the more difficult question of value. Robert McNamara was searching for *worth* when he introduced "bang for buck" concepts into defense management. He wanted to compare the offensive potential of a $10-million missile system with one costing $50 million. He recognized that worth had to be measured in terms of offensive power rather than dollars alone.

To understand worth a seller should know enough about the customer's business to predict how a price will be passed to the ultimate consumer. If the consumer is obligated to absorb all costs or has no choice in the matter, it will be easy for a supplier to get a high price. If, as happened to the printers' union several years ago, a high price forces publishers to close down newspapers, then it may prove self-defeating. The buyer should know how his purchase fits into the supplier's product-market plans. He may learn that the seller is less interested in immediate profit than in some other long-range goal.

Once buyers and sellers become committed to in-depth

worth and economic analysis they will be forced to cope with the following problems:

1. What is the "going concern" value of an asset or sale?

2. How can known and unknown risks be accounted for in an estimate or on the books?

3. How accurate or objective can an accounting record be?

4. What do expressions like "sunk cost," "opportunity cost," "tooling amortization," "depreciation" and "overhead" really mean?

5. How can costs in one period be related to accomplishments in another?

6. What is the appropriate measure of profitability in the long and short run? Is it return on costs, sales, investment or assets?

7. How are costs, profits and business volume related?

8. How should a new product be priced?

9. What does a purchased part really cost before it reaches the end user?

Men in accounting and cost-analysis have traditionally avoided these issues. They have also avoided the responsibility for relating product cost to product function. In the future they will be forced to accept these challenges, for an in-depth analysis of worth is indispensable to first-rate planning.

PRICE- AND COST-ANALYSIS

Price- and cost-analysis is an emerging profession. To do it properly requires discipline, imagination, modern statistical tools and common sense. The subject is too broad to be covered

briefly. Instead I shall make a few comments and recommendations based upon my management experience in product-pric-
ing on both the buying and selling sides of the business.

A price-analysis can be quite difficult. It would seem that
pricing a mattress would be rather simple, but it isn't. Once
somebody gets submerged in the problem and learns about
differences in materials, structure, price and warranty, the
complexities grow. Faced with the problem, my wife and I
bought the most expensive mattress that came with a twenty-
year unconditional warranty. After the purchase we realized
that one factor had been overlooked. We are in our forties and
failed to account for life-expectancy.

Industrial buyers have difficulty making price comparisons
even when they buy the same item. A purchase involving
twenty parts in March is not the same as one for two-hundred
parts in December. Aside from changes in technology, competition and price levels, some learning has usually intervened to
complicate the analysis.

Cost-analysis is more complex than price-analysis. Few
men in business have not been frustrated by the question "What
does it really cost?" Accountants are always able to come up
with a number and managers are always able to find reasons
why the number is wrong. Accounting records do not tell the
whole story even when items have been produced in reasonably
large quantities. When an item is new or unfamiliar, the cost
problem is indeed demanding.

Two methods exist for estimating production costs of new
equipment: one, statistical, involves making projections from
costs of similar equipment already in production; the second,
an industrial-engineering approach, involves making an estimate of the cost of each step in the process. Most estimating
of new products involves the second method.

In an industrial-engineering estimate the analyst is supposed to gain a clear understanding of what is being produced.
This normally involves a knowledge of specifications, fabrica-

tion processes and standards. From this information and some learning-curve theory it is presumably possible to estimate with reasonable accuracy. Unfortunately, reality intervenes. Estimators are not nearly as knowledgeable about specifications, processes or standards as we presume them to be. And even if they were, there is rarely enough time to do a decent job.

The statistical approach is even more crude because it requires the wisdom of a Solomon to divine just how complex one thing is when compared with another. It also rests on the assumption that the right relationships between cost and other characteristics can be found. For example, an analyst can assume that the cost of a rocket motor is proportional to its weight and horsepower. This may or may not be true depending on more factors than we understand. Cost-estimating is still in the dark ages.

Most companies continue to employ techniques that are little different from those used in the Civil War. Its practitioners are artists, not professionals. One may earn his license to practice with a shop background, a few magical words about learning curves and some common sense. Few practitioners have the engineering or economic background to do a disciplined analysis using modern tools.

It is always easier to describe problems than to find solutions. Here are a few suggestions that will improve the price- and cost-analysis capability of buyers and sellers:

1. Executives should demand a higher standard of analysis. The moment they raise their aspirations they will be rewarded by better analysis.

2. Professional engineers, economists and managerial accountants should be lured into the profession by offers of high pay and prestige.

3. Better estimating systems and communication links should be created to assure that contributors to an estimate understand its assumptions.

4. Probability-estimating using Monte Carlo simulation or equivalent methods should replace present single-point or "max-min" range estimates.

5. Statistical sampling and decision-making techniques should be utilized to a far greater degree.

6. Parametric estimating techniques should be developed by trained people who can understand its potential and limitations.

7. Estimating standards and data should be developed and saved with a view toward practical use and easy retrieval.

If a company desires to improve its cost-analysis capability as quickly as possible it should begin by following suggestions 1 and 2. A commitment to see the program through will facilitate the other recommendations. In time all aspects of the program will become operative and professional economic analysis a way of corporate life.

STRATEGIC DECISION-MAKING

Someone has to decide which strategic goals are important and which are not. When little is at stake and the issues simple, one man can decide; but when the negotiation is complex the decision becomes a group responsibility.

In the last analysis, groups do not have goals, but people within them do. Each person in the group tends to regard the issues from his own viewpoint and aspiration level. In the course of group interaction a negotiation takes place that results in what is commonly called "group objectives." It is power and bargaining skill, as well as *facts and assumptions,* which determine such matters as product-market mix, make or buy, the use of power, fact-finding methods and selection of the chief negotiator.

ASSUMPTIONS AND BOUNDED RATIONALITY

Decisions are inseparable from the assumptions upon which they are based. Few people stop to realize the degree to which assumptions play a part in their daily lives. I work and assume that a check will be given me on Friday. The bank assumes that I will give them the check on Monday. They then lend my money to businessmen on the assumption that I and others like me will not demand our money at once. These are, of course, reasonable assumptions. Or are they?

During the Depression many men didn't work, and others did but got only a small check on Friday. Instead of depositing money in the bank on Monday, they withdrew. The banks quickly ran out of funds and demanded repayment from businessmen, to whom they had loaned the money. The businessmen could not pay and were cut off from further help. They in turn stopped paying the employees, who ran to the bank, who ran to the businessmen—and the economy collapsed in a heap.

There is a principle of decision theory called "bounded rationality" meaning that human beings must make decisions without full information. Being limited in knowledge, tools and intelligence, they cannot find the optimum solution to a problem no matter how hard they try. This principle applies to the President of the United States as well as to you and me.

What people don't know may be a lot greater than what they know. We do a poor job estimating what others value and even find it hard to sort out our own value structure. When we search for solutions to problems we never look for all the possible alternatives. Instead we simplistically settle for the first satisfactory one and are thankful for having found it. If we come up with a few alternative solutions, we lack the tools or intelligence to figure out what would happen if we chose one. Since it is practical to arrive at some conclusion, we do the best we can with whatever information we possess. Unfortunately we have another big problem: we cannot see the future. Faced with this insurmountable obstacle, most of us think in a straight line. If things are going up, we predict they will go up; and if they are going down, we feel safe in pointing down. (It is this fallacy in judgment that makes most of us losers in the stock market.)

But, despite these limits to rationality, people make decisions. And they do it by making assumptions. Like an iceberg, some assumptions show, but most are hidden. Among the hidden assumptions we tend to make in decision-making are that the responsible committee members hold personal values which correspond to their corporate values; that they have searched for problem-solutions considerably beyond the few alternatives considered; and that they have evaluated the consequences of each alternative in an unbiased fashion. None of these hidden premises may be true.

Marshall McLuhan said that "any media has the power of imposing its own assumptions on the unwary." A standard lease, a loan application form and a certified profit-and-loss statement create assumptions of legitimacy that sometimes collapse under careful scrutiny.

Assumptions should be *identified* and *tested* throughout the negotiation process in much the same way that a scientist validates a theory. People who fail to do this become victims of their own bounded rationality. For instance, estimating in the aerospace industry is notoriously bad. We are in trouble on such big programs as the TFX fighter-bomber, the SST supersonic transport and the C5A. It's no wonder! At one company I watched a corporate officer cut a $12-million estimate to $5.8 million by changing the slope of a forecast line. Before the job ended, $53 million was spent. There was no cheating involved. Just poor assumptions about the state of the art.

STRATEGIC PLANNING AT HUGHES AIRCRAFT

The Hughes Aircraft Company does an excellent job of strategic planning in its major subcontract activity. An understanding of the system is important, as it brings to bear most of what we have discussed.

The key to Hughes' success in major purchases lies in its commitment to team decision-making and an early-warning information system. A Procurement Committee is organized years before a requirement is formalized in order to assure that overall company objectives are recognized.

The committee consists of members from engineering, pricing, quality, finance, program-management and purchasing. The group seeks to blend overall company needs with those of the individual functions. When trade-off conflicts arise they are surfaced and negotiated. The committee has responsibility for making strategic decisions in the following areas:

    a. Make or buy
    b. Prime contract and customer considerations
    c. Future potential
    d. Creation of maximum competition
    e. Technical limitations
    f. Funding and time limits
    g. Information and fact-finding control
    h. Supplier attitudes and relationships
    i. Product-market integration
    j. Worth- and risk-analysis
    k. Source evaluation

A subcontract manager serves as chief committee executive and negotiator throughout its life. His role is to maintain communications between members, to secure participation in decision-making and to plan the procurement from cradle to grave.

The committee convenes formally at least five times during its life.

1. When the procurement plan is submitted for ratification
2. Prior to issuance of proposal requests
3. Prior to source evaluation
4. When the source is selected
5. Prior to negotiation

The men learn to understand the aspirations of other team members and to respect their various skills long before negotiation takes place. Discussions with prospective suppliers are conducted with discretion in order to preserve bargaining power at a later date. The meetings also serve to acquaint the buyer with technical and risk aspects of the purchase. All told, a climate of negotiation is created in which sensible long-range decisions can be made.

Management systems do not always work the way they are supposed to, but this one works well. Information to and from suppliers is carefully controlled. Members serve as communication links in an information-gathering chain. Auditors, instead of worrying entirely about overhead and labor rates, become concerned with the adequacy of control systems and supplier profit forecasts. Cost-analysts perform on-site studies and bring back information about deficiencies in scheduling and quality. Engineering contacts are viewed as an opportunity to better understand the supplier's personality, perceptions and goals.

The Hughes system is far from flawless. There are times when personalities clash and team leaders prove inadequate. Too many occasions arise where specialists dominate the committee and make a farce of the proceedings. Time and talent are rarely adequate to provide first-rate worth- and cost-analysis. Chief negotiators are not selected with the care that such large purchases deserve. While these deficiencies are not minor, the system works well. Two Hughes executives, W. A. Van Allen and T. Kotsovolos, deserve credit for seeing the need years ago for an effective method of purchasing in an age of change. It was a sound move.

Before attention is directed to tactics, a few words should be said to sellers and buyers individually. Throughout this chapter the point has been made that the strategic-planning problems of both are, for practical purposes, similar. However, there are differences that merit consideration.

A SPECIAL WORD TO THE SELLER

It doesn't do a bit of good to plan for a negotiation that never occurs. Therefore an important step in the seller's plan is to assure that one takes place. The following suggestions are to the point:

1. A proposal is never the best possible, for it represents a compromise based on time and energy limitations. The interest of *both* parties is served if the seller reviews the proposal after submittal. Invariably he will find that some requirements have been overlooked and that part of the submittal requires clarification.

2. Changes to a proposal are perfectly proper. The seller should feel free to ask the customer if the submittal is responsive and what can be done to clarify its intent.

3. A negotiated purchase is not the same as an advertised or low-bidder purchase. In a negotiated procurement it is permissible for a buyer to inform the supplier that his price is considered too high. It is also permissible for a seller to change his proposal in response to information developed at the negotiation.

4. A seller should monitor the proposal after submittal. Although buyers are not supposed to discuss status, some do.

In any case, information can sometimes be obtained from discussions with specialists, auditors and cost analysts, whose presence in the supplier's plant is in itself good news.

5. Unspoken signs of regard should be noted. Casual remarks, attitudes, glances and gestures may be as revealing as firm statements.

6. A supplier who invests time with the customer's engineering and purchasing people early in the specification stage usually receives a dividend at source-selection time.

7. A seller must be *thoroughly* familiar with his proposal and have back-up available. I have seen cases where back-up was actually lost, and others in which the back-up had very little relevance to the submitted price. It is not an easy matter to back into a set of figures on a complex proposal, and some people do a poor job of it. In their rush to accomplish some other pressing matter they overlook this critical responsibility.

8. A seller should invest substantial time in three areas: 1) a sound estimating system, 2) a sound cost-accounting system and 3) competent, analytical pricing specialists. The best defense against the buyer's negotiation assault is a price based on data accumulated in a businesslike way.

9. The seller knows more about his product and cost structure than the buyer is ever likely to know. This important source of power should not be forgotten or dismissed lightly.

These suggestions are but a few that apply to the seller in particular. At many schools of business administration, marketing and purchasing are taught together. This is as it should be, as the best preparation for the seller may well be a thorough knowledge of his customer's product-market structure and buying methods.

A SPECIAL WORD TO THE BUYER

When I was a young man I got a job in a stationery store for $12 a week. The first thing the owner taught me was that "the customer is always right." An important step in the buyer's plan is to assure that he is right. The following recommendations may be of value:

1. In most cases the buyer is in a powerful position. This power should be preserved and enhanced *throughout* the buying process.

2. Whether or not it is real, competition is a source of power. If the supplier believes that competition exists, then for practical purposes, competition exists.

3. The buyer's objective throughout the pre-award cycle is to learn all he can about the seller's goals, values, organization and product. Conversely, the less the seller knows about the buyer, the better.

4. A buyer must know what he is buying, which is not always easy. Unless somebody on the team knows the product, it is not really possible to do a good negotiation job.

5. Because a seller knows more about his costs and product than the customer, it is imperative that the customer defend himself. The buyer should put the best talent possible to work on understanding a seller's worth, cost and product-market structure.

6. In many industries, and especially the aerospace industry, estimating and cost systems are not good. Astute cost- and engineering-analysis can reveal soft spots in a supplier's proposal, especially when the work involves multiple divisions and processes. A buyer is wise to assume that the seller's estimating system is bad and then proceed to find out just how bad it really is.

7. A *talented* cost analyst and engineering partner can usually learn more by spending a few days in a supplier's plant than by looking at proposal figures for a month.

8. A supplier is reluctant to discuss technical risk for fear

he will not get the order. Realistic risk-taking and risk-identifi-
cation are major elements of buying and negotiation. The buyer
must probe to uncover this mutually unpleasant aspect of
procurement.

9. Many buyers are still confused in their thinking about
negotiated purchases; the government is not. Armed Services Procurement Regulation 3-805.1(b), below, represents a
sensible policy for commercial industry.

> Whenever negotiations are conducted with more than one
> offeror, auction techniques are strictly prohibited; an ex-
> ample would be indicating to an offeror a price which
> must be met to obtain further consideration, or informing
> him that his price is not low in relation to that of another
> offeror. On the other hand, it is permissible to inform an
> offeror that his price is considered by the Government to be
> too high. After receipt of proposals, no information regarding
> the number or identity of the offerors participating in the
> negotiations shall be made available to the public or to
> anyone whose official duties do not require such knowl-
> edge. Whenever negotiations are conducted with several
> offerors, while such negotiations may be conducted suc-
> cessively, all offerors selected to participate in such nego-
> tiations . . . shall be offered an equitable opportunity to
> submit such price, technical, or other revisions in their
> proposals as may result from the negotiations. All such
> offerors shall be informed of the specified date . . . of the
> closing of negotiations and that any revisions to their pro-
> posals must be submitted by that date. In addition, all such
> offerors shall also be informed that after the specified date
> for the closing of negotiation no information other than
> notice of unacceptability of proposal . . . will be furnished
> to any offeror until award has been made.

On the surface the above comments are relevant primarily to professional retail and industrial buyers. In point of
fact all who buy are affected. Those who scoff at this should
try to buy custom stereo or scuba-diving equipment. It almost
requires an engineering degree to make the proper risk-cost-
quality trade-offs. Whether we like it or not, consumers will be
wise to become more professional in their approach to buying
and negotiation.

CLIENTS AND ATTORNEYS

Attorneys have asked about the applicability of the planning model to their work. The strategic decisions described in this chapter are as relevant to them as to anyone who negotiates. A lawyer must decide what his product-market specialty is and pursue his opportunities accordingly. It is no longer possible to specialize in divorce, personal injury, estate-planning and criminal law and perform effectively in each area. There is simply too much to know and too much to keep up with for a man to do everything well.

Although fee-splitting is frowned upon it does go on for sound economic reasons. If these reasons did not exist, fee-splitting would soon stop. Whenever a lawyer gets a case that is outside his specialty area he must consider farming out all or some of the work to other attorneys or investigators. This is no different from the make-or-buy decision made by company executives.

Decision-making relationships are certainly of strategic importance. Unless the attorney for the insurance company is familiar with the policies and executive structure of his client, he may find himself battling client and plaintiff or acting as a messenger boy between them.

There is really no part of the strategic-decision process shown in Table 4 that is not applicable to the attorney. Attitude-structuring is of concern because the lawyer meets insurance-company personnel, attorneys and judges on case after case. He must balance the needs of a client against his own long-range interests. The question of power, fact-finding and ethical standards must be analyzed before negotiations begin. Unless this is done the full leverage of knowledge, uncertainty, reward and potential litigation will be improperly used.

While we have emphasized the anatomy of time from a buy-sell standpoint, nowhere does time carry so much weight as in legal work. This is especially true in personal-injury cases, the fastest-growing segment of the legal profession. Every action of the injured party and the insurance company at each point in the cycle is pertinent to achieving a satisfactory settlement. Cost-risk trade-offs during the presuit, postsuit, preverdict and postverdict phases of negotiation should be understood by lawyer and client. We may conclude that strategic needs of attorneys and businessmen are more alike than different.

CONCLUSION

Strategic planning is the cornerstone of effective negotiation. One does not prepare a plan while sitting at the bargaining table in today's world. The negotiator and his organization must know where they want to go and why before detailed tactics can be selected.

Lewis Carroll wrote in *Through the Looking-Glass*, "Now here you see, it takes all the running you can do, to keep in the same place. If you want to get somewhere else, you must run at least twice as fast as that!" Good strategic planning is one way to run "twice as fast as that" in the age of complexity. Without such a plan the negotiator is like a sailor without a course. He will be driven wherever the winds blow and use most of his energy just to stay afloat.

CHAPTER 14

TACTICS,
DEADLOCK AND
COUNTERMEASURES

TACTICS: THE SCIENCE AND ART OF DISPOSING AND MANEU-
VERING FORCES IN COMBAT; THE ART OR SKILL OF EMPLOY-
ING AVAILABLE MEANS TO ACCOMPLISH AN END

Webster

WHERE ENDS ARE AGREED, THE ONLY QUESTIONS LEFT ARE
THOSE OF MEANS, AND THESE ARE NOT POLITICAL BUT
TECHNICAL, THAT IS TO SAY, CAPABLE OF BEING SETTLED BY
EXPERTS.

Isaiah Berlin

EVERY MEANS TENDS TO BECOME AN END.

Ignazio Silone

Senator McGovern believes that the strategic question in
Vietnam is whether Americans should ever be involved in a
shooting war on the Asian mainland. As far as he is concerned
we should not. He therefore insists that our tactics at the peace
table are entirely wrong.

President Johnson believed that our military presence in
Vietnam would assure the vitality of democratic institutions

in Southeast Asia and was determined to win that objective through a policy of negotiation backed by force. He therefore employed "talk-fight" tactics consistent with enemy pressures and his strategic decision. Whether President Nixon fundamentally agrees with the strategy of Senator McGovern or that of Lyndon Johnson will not be clear for several years.

The tactics we are using in Paris seem to be based on warnings provided by Admiral C. Turner Joy fifteen years earlier.[26] For ten months the Admiral sat opposite the Communists in Korea. Afterward, in his book, *How Communists Negotiate,* he made a number of recommendations, some of which have been employed by ambassadors Harriman and Lodge.

1. No American concession should be made without an equivalent Communist response. The Communists should not be permitted unilaterally to choose the conference site nor should it be in their area of control.

2. The American team should be staffed with clear and rapid-thinking negotiators of the highest quality.

3. Americans must be ready to use threat of force and to implement such threat if necessary.

4. Integrity on the part of the Communists should not be assumed.

5. Conferences should be brief and conducted within pre-established time limits.

The Admiral's suggestions would make little sense to Senator McGovern but fit in nicely with President Johnson's strategic concept.

The choice of tactics is limited by strategy. It does little good to win a short-run gain if a long-range goal is violated.

In the business world a seller who employs "low-balling" maneuvers soon gets a bad reputation and loses customers. The job of the chief negotiator is to tie all the important considerations together and come up with tactics that satisfy long-range objectives. In doing so he must define the issues, problems and subgoals. He must inoculate the team against persuasion. Finally, he must decide how best to test the assumptions, intentions and aspirations of the opponent through the use of maneuvers and techniques.

MANEUVERS

Tactics can be divided into two areas, maneuvers and techniques. A maneuver is not a strategy. If we were speaking of military tactics, a maneuver would be described as a movement designed to secure a position of advantage for offensive or defensive purposes. A negotiation maneuver is a move designed to create a situation in which goals can be reached and bargaining positions defended.

Not all maneuvers are ethical. Those that are not have no place in our society. Those in the gray area between right and wrong should be looked at with healthy skepticism. The fact remains, however, that there are people whose standard of integrity is so distorted that anything is acceptable. I have negotiated with men in the movie business whose ethics were so low that their every move had to be guarded against like a disease. To protect ourselves it is necessary to understand both ethical and unethical maneuvers and to recognize when they are being employed by an opponent. In order to do this I have classified maneuvers into seven categories shown in Table 4. They are: 1) timing, 2) inspection, 3) association, 4) authority, 5) amount, 6) brotherhood and 7) detours.

NEGOTIATION MANEUVERS. Table 4

TIMING

Patience
Deadline
Speed
Fait accompli
Surprise
Status quo
Stretchout

INSPECTION

Open inspection
Limited inspection
Confession
Qualified
Third party
No admittance

ASSOCIATION

Alliances
Associates
Disassociates
United Nations
Bribery

AUTHORITY

Limited authority
Approval
Escalation approval
Missing man
Arbitration

AMOUNT

Fair and reasonable
Bulwarism
Nibbling
Budget bogy
Blackmail
Escalation
Intersection
Non-negotiable
Chinese Auction

BROTHERHOOD

Equal brothers
Big brother
Little brother
Long-lost brothers
Brinkmanship

DETOUR

Decoy
Denial
Withdrawal
Good and bad guys
False statistics and errors
Scrambled eggs
Low-balling
Scoundrel

TIMING (SETTING THE TEMPO OF EVENTS)

Time maneuvers are important because they are a basic source of power. Events governing time may be real or imaginary. In either case time limits do not exist for practical bargaining purposes unless they are thought to be credible.

People in industrial societies are tied to the hidden language of the clock. When someone says, "I've got to catch a plane at five," we know exactly what he means. The same is true when a buyer says that he will place an order with a supplier by the following morning. Of the seven maneuvers shown below, three, patience, stretchout and deadline, are especially important. The others, with the exception of *fait accompli,* are self-explanatory and will not be elaborated upon.

1. Patience (willing to bear with the situation)
2. Deadline (limits)
3. Speed (quick agreements)
4. *Fait accompli* (accomplished and irreversible)
5. Surprise (take unawares)
6. Status quo (static and changeless condition)
7. Stretchout (delay until uncertainty is reduced)

Patience requires the maturity to withstand immediate satisfaction in exchange for the expectation of gaining more in the future. Most people have a strong need to end the tension imposed by negotiation as quickly as possible. As we have seen in the experiment, quick negotiations do not generate good settlements.

A special form of the patience maneuver is the *stretchout* maneuver. In this case a deliberate decision is made by one party to extend the negotiations over a long period of time so that some of the known and unknown uncertainties will reveal themselves prior to final agreement. The government sometimes gives a contractor a letter go-ahead and then takes as long as one or two years to definitize the agreement. A stretchout negotiation should be accepted by a supplier only after a rational consideration of its fairness.

Deadline is a powerful maneuver because it imposes the possibility of real loss upon both parties. In auto negotiations it is not uncommon to have a series of deadlines associated with such matters as contract expiration, strike votes and actual strike. The strange thing about deadline is that people so often accept somebody else's deadline as their own, despite the fact that time limits have a way of imposing a discipline on both parties that can favor one more than the other. In Chapter 1, Starmatic was foolish to begin negotiations at the time requested by the buyer. Not only was Starmatic unprepared, but it forfeited an easy opportunity to test relative bargaining strength. It was no accident that so many agreements were reached in the last five minutes of the experiment or that Ho Chi Minh consented to serious peace talks a few days before the election in 1968. Deadline, whether real or imaginary, can precipitate decision.

The *fait accompli* maneuver is relatively unfamiliar to businessmen but well known to diplomats. When one country takes over the territory of another in a surprise attack and then negotiates from this strong position, they are using this maneuver. Lawyers employ the same idea when they tie up a defendant's large bank account prior to a hearing involving a much lesser amount. Once some things are done, they can become important realities of bargaining power. This is true regardless of whether the action taken is legal. The expression "Possession is nine-tenths of the law" is to the point.

INSPECTION (EXAMINATION AND VERIFICATION)

In negotiation, the question of truth is always a factor. Both parties present arguments that require substantiation. Credibility can be enhanced in a variety of ways. For example, when a buyer is advised that he may review a seller's books, the effect is to increase his faith in the integrity of the seller's position.

The six maneuvers below are used to establish a bargaining climate consistent with the strategic need for security and the tactical need for credibility.

1. Open inspection (full freedom to examine)

2. Limited inspection (controlled access)
3. Confession (full disclosure)
4. Qualified confession (limited answers to questions)
5. Third party (access to records by neutral parties)
6. No admittance (complete security of records)

ASSOCIATION ("FRIENDS AND ENEMIES")

In a negotiation it makes sense to find third parties who are friends. Bargaining power can be strengthened by various association maneuvers.

1. Alliances (strong partners)
2. Associates (friends)
3. Disassociates (mutual nonfriends)
4. United Nations (broad-based alliance of interested parties)
5. Bribery (payoff and collusion)

The *bribery* maneuver deserves special attention because it is so difficult to pin down. Artie Samish, a California lobbyist of the forties, bragged that he could get any law passed with "bribes, broads or baked potatoes." He spoke once too often and was put away. The three B's are a reality that every business must defend against. Few who give or take bribes are as foolish as Artie, who added a fourth B, bragging.

AUTHORITY (DECISION-MAKERS)

Years ago I read in *Life* that the Skouras brothers used the authority maneuver to good advantage in movie negotiations. When an agent bargained against the Skouras organization he started with the youngest brother. After the two had been at it for a long while and reached a tentative agreement, the next older brother was asked to approve. He refused and then proceeded to bargain on his own authority. The process was then repeated with Spyros himself. Few agents had the stamina and dedication to withstand such an onslaught. It is well to remember that the authority to make a final decision can be used effectively for getting or *not* getting a job done. These maneuvers are to the point:

1. Limited authority (restricted right to make final decision)
2. Approval (mandatory approval designed to impede agreement)
3. Escalating approval (deliberate imposition of sequential higher-approval veto)
4. Missing man (deliberate absence of person with final authority)
5. Arbitration (third-party decision, impartial or biased)

Few negotiators have not at one time or another been surprised by unforseen authority problems. The fact that a man has limited authority may prove to be an opportunity rather than a problem. Local claims managers in the insurance business take pride in settling claims. They may at times prefer to settle at a point close to their upper limit rather than pass the file to a higher authority.

Perhaps the best way to avoid authority surprises is to ask the adversary to state his organizational status and authority limits early in the session. Another method is to determine, on the basis of past performance, if others have had authority problems with the opponent. In either case, nothing is foolproof. Authority surprises will continue to occur whenever someone wants them to.

AMOUNT (PRICE, QUANTITY OR DEGREE)

There are many ways to reach a goal. A negotiator can state his price and say, "Take it or leave it," or he can "nibble" away at the opponent. He can appeal to fairness or resort to blackmail to win his ends. Nine variations of the *amount* maneuver occur with relative frequency.

1. Fair and reasonable (equitable)
2. Bulwarism (take it or leave it)
3. Nibbling (take in small bits at a time)
4. Budget bogy (tailor package to price)
5. Blackmail (pay or else)
6. Escalation (ever-increasing demands)
7. Intersection (simultaneous negotiation of multiple and divergent contracts)
8. Non-negotiable (exorbitant demands for the purpose of creating deadlock)
9. Chinese Auction (the competitive-negotiation crunch)

Of the above, several may be unfamiliar. *Bulwarism* occurs when one party, who is unwilling to make any but minor changes, starts by making a final offer to the other. For many years General Electric used this "take it or leave it" approach against the electrical workers with mixed results. The *intersection* maneuver seeks to tie existing and future contracts into the content of ongoing negotiations. In Paris we are attempting to achieve a military and political settlement in Vietnam while considering the neutralization of all Southeast Asia. In a large company, two buyers can deal with the same supplier without knowing it. If negotiations can be made to intersect, the leverage of one may extend to the other.

Escalation is a tricky maneuver that works like this. After two parties come to an agreement, one of them raises his demand. Hitler worked this trick on Chamberlain to good effect. In my experiment, seven negotiators demanded $2 million rather than the $1,075,000 specified in the instructions. They did very well compared with the average. Occasionally a seller in the aerospace business decides to raise his proposal price immediately prior to conference. The buyer is usually taken aback and finds himself fighting desperately to achieve the original price rather than some lower target. The reason for escalation may be legitimate or purely tactical. A wise negotiator will recognize the maneuver and refuse to accept its premises.

Two other maneuvers are of practical interest. The *budget bogy* maneuver is used by buyers on the basis of its surface legitimacy. The seller is faced with a fixed dollar amount, which becomes a focal point. If the budget constraint is accepted by the seller, he is then forced to reduce the price and scope of work.

A seller should never accept the assumption that a budget is firm without testing the premise and learning why another source of funding is unavailable. Most budgets are more flexible than they look. Large amounts can sometimes be shifted from account to account by a clever controller if the pressure to do so is maintained. An apparently firm constraint can fade away if the budget period can be reshaped by time and purpose.

The amazing part of the budget maneuver is that sellers too often bring this plight upon themselves. A buyer or engineer asks the seller for some approximation of the cost months before the final design or quantity is determined. The seller, anxious to please, states a figure and thereafter boxes himself in because the buyer incorporates the amount into his product-market mix. One is reminded of Shakespeare's line in *Hamlet*, "Words without thoughts never to heaven go." Prices submitted for a buyer's planning purpose too often are "words without thoughts."

The *Chinese Auction* maneuver has overtones that, while ethical, are at the very least severe. In this maneuver the buyer negotiates with two or three suppliers so that each knows that the others are being considered favorably. A few years ago I faced this maneuver in a blatant form. I was one of three suppliers in an open bullpen waiting to go into the negotiating room. The feeling was unpleasant, especially so because the potential order was large and our work backlog low.

The only countermeasure for this maneuver is a thorough analysis of the power structure and first-rate interorganizational communications. A negotiator must have the courage of his convictions and test the opponent as though competition were not so apparent. He may find that the buyer's bias will reveal itself and thereby provide a working signal by which tactics can be changed.

BROTHERHOOD (REASONING TOGETHER)

Basic buyer-supplier attitudes and relationships are specified by strategy. However, it is the negotiator's job to develop a marriage of interests and values between parties. Some degree of brotherhood, however tenuous, must be established if the parties are to do business.

Brothers are not necessarily equal, nor do they take care of each other in the same way. It may or may not be wise to play the part of big brother or equal brother. Of the five variations in this category, four are self-explanatory, and the last, brinkmanship, has been discussed in Chapter 6.

1. Equal brothers (based on equal status)
2. Big brother (benevolence based on higher status)
3. Little brother (charity desired on basis of lower status)
4. Long-lost brothers (search for relationship and status)
5. Brinkmanship (intersecting destinies based on high joint risk)

DETOUR (DIVERSIONS)

Negotiation is a difficult business. It is essential to learn all you can about the opponent while letting him know as little as necessary about yourself. To do this, detour maneuvers of one kind or another are employed. Of the eight listed, several are unmistakably unethical. While unethical maneuvers should never be condoned, they must be understood if the negotiator is to protect himself.

1. Decoys (attractor or snare)
2. Denial (negation or retraction of statement)
3. Withdrawal (false attack and retreat)
4. Good and bad guys ("sugar and spice" role-playing)
5. False statistics and errors (creating figures that deceive)
6. Scrambled eggs (creating deliberate confusion of issues and figures)
7. Low-balling (exploitation by deliberate add-ons and changes)
8. Scoundrel (deliberate larceny by never-ending re-negotiation)

Maneuvers five through eight should be explained briefly. In the heat of bargaining things can get very complicated even with the best of intentions. With the worst of intentions errors in arithmetic and statistics can be deliberate and misleading. The *false-statistics* maneuver is dangerous because it is so subtle. Numbers are fine, but the assumptions behind them are often dubious.

Scrambled eggs represents a deliberate attempt to complicate rather than simplify the transaction for the purpose of creating confusion. A man must have the self-confidence and courage to say that he doesn't know what is going on or he will find himself agreeing to something foolish.

Low-balling is a maneuver based on "fooling" the opponent into an apparent agreement with the intention of raising the price after he is lured into the trap. Auto salesmen are infamous for low-balling customers into extras and exorbitant finance charges. I know a high-class low-baller who was a marketing vice-president. He made agreements with the government at low prices with the *deliberate intention* of eliminating his competition and profiting later by *forcing* costly specification changes.

Scoundrel is a maneuver that is strictly unethical. In this world some people are so twisted that they take advantage of others in any way they can. To understand the scoundrel is to be on guard against him. The maneuver consists of a negotiation that never ends. The scoundrel's idea is to lure his opponent into a deal by making an especially attractive offer. Once the opponent is mentally committed to reaching an agreement and has discarded consideration of other competitors, the process begins in earnest.

The scoundrel makes and breaks verbal agreements with impunity. The methods used for repudiating agreement vary, but often include disapproval by higher authority, inability to clarify terms, misunderstanding, transcription problems, errors in figures, legal delays and missing-man games. The scoundrel is careful to maintain cordial relations until a contract is signed. Unless his opponent is sharp, words and figures undergo a subtle transformation at contract time. The opponent, upon signing, breaths a sigh of relief despite the fact that he is not nearly as well off as he thought he would be. Poor fool! His troubles have barely begun, for he has yet to face the despair of breach, legal delay, insults, endless debate, double bookkeeping and costs for judgments that are likely to prove uncollectable.

What has been described happens every day to men who are foolish, greedy or unlucky. Few have the wealth or fortitude to fight the scoundrel. The best advice in dealing with these exploiters is to run the other way at the *first* sign of bad faith. If running is impossible, the only alternative is to get help from the best lawyers, accountants and technical specialists in town.

THE NEED FOR FLEXIBILITY

Maneuvers considered appropriate at the start of a conference may prove unsuitable as new information develops. A negotiator should maintain a flexible attitude throughout the meeting by questioning his tactics in a disciplined manner. The points suggested below should be considered in the reevaluation:

1. Should maneuvers be changed or combined differently at this stage in the talks?

2. Are there any penalties associated with unethical or shady practices? Should there be any?

3. How will a particular maneuver be interpreted by the opponent at this point in the discussion? Will it destroy a desirable long-range relationship? Will it make the point you really want it to make?

Proper selection of tactical maneuvers does not guarantee success, but the negotiator who is attuned to their use and ready to make adjustments can better defend his objectives than the man who "plays it by ear."

TECHNIQUES

Techniques are the fine-tuning mechanism by which goals are reached. Among the most familiar techniques are agenda, questions, concessions, commitments, threats, deadlock and nonverbal communication. As Table 5 indicates, there are many

---

NEGOTIATION TECHNIQUES. Table 5

---

1. Agenda
2. Questions
3. Statements
4. Concessions
5. Commitments
6. Moves
7. Threats
8. Promises
9. Recess
10. Delays
11. Deadlock
12. Focal points
13. Standards

14. Secrecy measures
15. Nonverbal communications
16. Media choices
17. Listening
18. Caucus
19. Formal and informal memorandum
20. Informal discussions
21. Trial balloons and leaks
22. Hostility relievers
23. Temporary intermediaries
24. Location of negotiation
25. Technique of time

methods available to the astute bargainer. The balance of this chapter will be devoted to an analysis of the most familiar techniques.

Techniques are not grand strategy. They are, in a sense, weapons in an arsenal. If well employed, they provide a source of power at the table. If poorly conceived, they can be counter-productive and create needless hostility. It therefore makes sense that we know as much about them as possible.

AGENDA, ISSUES AND PROBLEMS

On Saturday, January 18, 1969, there appeared in the *Los Angeles Times* a dispatch from Saigon to the effect that the United States was prepared to propose an agenda. In order of importance the issues to be discussed were 1) cease-fire in the demilitarized zone, 2) prisoner exchange and 3) troop-withdrawal. The dispatch concluded: "Privately U.S. Diplomats view such an agenda as a bargaining ploy akin to opening demands of a labor union at contract negotiation time." The first major test in Paris, as in other negotiations, is the agenda. It represents the first step by which an opponent's expectations, attitudes and values can be formally evaluated.

The best way to look at agenda is along lines suggested by the ideas of Marshall McLuhan. Agenda is media. Like all media it has the power to shape a message and tell a story of its own. It is more than a mere listing of acts in a vaudeville show. Rather, it is a reflection of the power of the parties and the importance of issues.

Agenda can be designed to play a specific role in negotiations. It can clarify or hide motives. It can establish rules that are fair or biased. It can keep negotiations on the track or permit easy digression. An agenda can be simply a program of items to be discussed or it can be coordinated with other maneuvers and techniques. For example, agenda items in labor negotiations are sometimes organized so that discussions of difficult issues occur at the precise time that a strike vote is to be taken or a not-so-wild "wildcat" strike begins.

We know from our discussion of persuasion theory in Chapter 1 that the organization of argument and media are important where message acceptance is desired. An agenda can introduce the best arguments and speakers where the effect will be strongest. It can also facilitate agreement on difficult issues by arranging that the discussion begin with matters that are less controversial.

Although it can easily be seen that issues and problems are the heart of agenda, it is not so obvious that rules of negotiation may be shaped by it. In Paris the Saigon government insisted for some time that they would not respond to any direct communication from the Viet Cong. To them it was a major issue because the *rule* implied an important relationship between the parties. Rules of discussion can be sources of power based on legitimacy and must therefore be analyzed by both parties before acceptance.

A carefully thought out agenda forces a decision as to which issues and problems are worth talking about. From a tactical standpoint, I believe that it is generally best to test the goals and intentions of an opponent by introducing a large number of issues rather than few. An opponent may prove to be less interested in some points than you assumed he was. Furthermore, the approach tends to dampen his expectations and aspirations. It is sometimes easy to forget that issues, real or imaginary, have trading value in the bargaining process. They can be exchanged for something else.

The rule for introducing problems into the agenda is simple: put them where they can best be solved. In general, those that can be solved easily deserve priority, for they generate a climate of success. Because problem-solving depends upon open discussion and value-sharing, the agenda should also consider whether problems should be solved at a different place and time than bitterly fought issues. It might be wise, for example, to let the financial people resolve audit problems in a special conference where matters of this nature can be discussed quietly. The solution can then be brought to the table as a step toward general agreement. A problem of this delicate nature might generate enormous heat if left to the give-and-take of conference debate.

Diplomats tend to look at agenda as a serious matter because of its impact on rules, assumptions and issues. Businessmen can ill afford to treat it lightly, but more often than not do.

CONCESSION AND COMPROMISE

Several thousand men died before Hanoi or Washington made the initial concession regarding whether peace talks would be held in Warsaw or Honolulu. Our experiment found that losers make the first concession in a negotiation. Whether a first concession in this matter was worth the price is a question of strategy, not tactics.

Concession has four purposes: 1) to determine *what* the

opponent wants, 2) how *much* he wants, 3) how *badly* and 4) what he is *willing to give up* to get what he wants. It is a technique for testing preconference assumptions about the opponent.

In 1960, two psychologists concluded that the "ideal" bargainer had high aspirations, opened with a high demand and made smaller concessions than his opponent. Our experiment confirmed these findings. It appears that the "ideal" concession pattern is an effective test of an opponent's intentions.

Several writers have debated the question of initial offer and its relationship to first concession. They have suggested that three opening buyer gambits deserve consideration:

1. Reveal no initial position.
2. Reveal a minimum position.
3. Reveal both minimum and target position.

In my opinion, the first approach is by far best, but unfortunately sellers are rarely nice enough to let a negotiator get away without revealing an initial position. A little bit of thought about the third position reveals that it is patently absurd since it assumes that a buyer can easily retreat from a higher offer (target) to a lower if the seller ungraciously refuses to accept the higher offer.

The second position deserves careful thought because it is deceptive. If a negotiator is serious about achieving his minimum position, he would be insane to open with that figure. Once the minimum is stated at the outset, an opponent has every reason to believe that he can do somewhat better. It is safe to say that the best opening gambit is an offer below the desired minimum, provided it has a degree of logic behind it. Wherever possible, one should be prepared to concede something in the course of a negotiation. On the other hand, the opponent should be forced to work for everything he gets.

This brings us to the question "Does one concession deserve another?" The traditional American attitude toward compromise carries over into bargaining. Most of us tend to feel that one good deed deserves another. I believe we would be wise to question our normal instincts in this matter of reciprocity. Just because an adversary makes a concession and expects something in return is no reason to respond in kind.

When an opponent makes a concession, the negotiator has several options. He may concede less or more than the other party. He may concede something immediately or promise something in the future. He may grant a small, unimportant concession on one issue in exchange for a major point. He may choose to concede nothing, promise nothing and merely continue to talk. He may decide to be clear in his response or deliberately obscure. The important thing to remember is that each reply is valid from a tactical standpoint and represents a different degree of reciprocity.

Concession is one area in which good theory and good practice merge. Each concession has an effect on the aspiration level of the opponent and is at the same time a reflection of the negotiator's own resolve to meet his objectives. The amount, the rate and the rate of change of concession are critical factors. One should never compromise on any point without thought of future consequences.

COMMITMENT

Every concession implies a degree of commitment or willingness to stand firm. The "doorknob," or "deal point," price tells the opponent he has only two choices: accept the last offer or allow negotiations to break down. In either case the final decision becomes entirely the responsibility of the opponent. For most people this is an overwhelming emotional experience.

The difficulty with a "doorknob" price is that the opponent may not believe it. Careful analysis must therefore be directed to how a believable commitment can be made. Several methods are available. Credibility can be created by behavior that makes retreat difficult. If, for example, a negotiator's behavior is related to public announcement of a position or to some recognized standard or principle, then the opponent can see for himself that retreat from the position is impossible without loss of face.

It is possible to phrase a commitment so that it sounds final but permits the negotiator to retreat gracefully if necessary. The answer lies in finding a method that will obscure the phrase in some way. This can be accomplished by varying four factors: 1) content (referring precisely to what is covered by the phrase), 2) firmness (referring to the certainty with which final action will be taken), 3) consequences (referring to the specific final action promised) and 4) time (referring to the precise time of the final action promised). An example will help us understand this better.

The statement "I cannot accept your clause and will walk out immediately if you do not change it" differs from "It is not possible for me to accept the $100-a-day charge in your clause. I will return to my management unless we can resolve the matter." Both are commitments that sound firm but are in fact obscure. In the first the reference may be either to the entire clause or some part of it. In the second the elements of time, consequences and firmness are, to a degree, unclear.

Commitment is a two-edged sword. If it is believed, agreement follows; if not, bargaining position is weakened. The *exact* wording of a commitment is therefore of practical importance. Whether the commitment technique will be productive or counterproductive depends upon how skillfully its use is planned.

QUESTIONS AND ANSWERS

Several years ago I was a member of a management audit team whose mission it was to investigate an operating department. We began by interviewing key executives. To our surprise the men unhesitatingly answered questions and led us to problem areas that might otherwise never have been uncovered. We learned that the less we spoke, the more they did. The less evaluative we were regarding their answers, the more critical they were of themselves. When I discussed this with a friend in psychiatry, he was not surprised. People enjoy answering questions about themselves and their work even when some of the material is unpleasant. They want to be heard.

We are victimized by the school system as far as negotiation questions and answers are concerned. School success is based largely upon giving correct answers. The more facts remembered and regurgitated, the higher the grade. When a question is asked in school, it is good to answer correctly and bad not to. However, in negotiation, correct answers are not necessarily good and are often quite stupid.

The art of answering questions in negotiation lies in knowing what to answer and what not to; when to be clear and when not to. It does not lie in being right or wrong.

With this background we can proceed to analyze questions specifically in terms of the man who asks and the man who answers. From the standpoint of the questioner, several suggestions are appropriate. First, it is generally wise to ask a question even when it appears to be a bit personal, or even ridiculous. The questioner may be rewarded with a better answer than he believes possible, or may learn something from a negative response. Second, the purpose of a question is to find out about an opponent's values, assumptions and intentions. Questions should not be designed to show how smart a negotiator is or how stupid his opponent may be. Third, the Perry Mason concept of interrogation appears to me inappropriate to negotiation and likely to be counterproductive. A man should not be trapped into an answer. I have seen men play lawyer and convert the session into a battleground for no purpose but to serve their egos. Psychological research indicates that questions asked in a supportive climate are more apt to elicit useful answers. Most investigators conclude that people placed in a defensive position withhold information and tend to distort what they hear and what they say. Fourth, it is best to keep questions simple. A great deal can be learned from answers that explain where, who, what, which, why, when and how.

From the viewpoint of the person who answers a question, the following thoughts may be useful. First, not all questions need be answered. Many questions are asked for which no answer is possible; others are asked without expectation of reply. The correct answer is one that is related to the strategic plan and not to the questioner's purpose. A negotiation conference is not a classroom, nor is it a place to please the other party by being accommodating.

Second, a negotiator should frame his answers as a politician does. The wise politician is aware of his party's platform and knows how to integrate the needs of local constituents to the overall program. Bargainers who do not have a clearly definitized strategic plan will find themselves in the embarrassing position of providing answers that violate their long-range objectives.

THREAT

By its very nature, negotiation involves a degree of threat. The fact that rewards can be withheld or punishment inflicted by deadlock constitutes a threat. The central question that confronts the bargainer is not whether threat will be used as a tactic, but whether an emphasis on open threat is beneficial. The answer depends on four factors: 1) strategic plan, 2) relative ability to punish, 3) threat credibility and 4) the size of the threat.

The use of threat should be geared to strategic needs. What makes sense for one strategy may be insane for another. President Nixon made it clear to the Russians that his stand in favor of the antiballistic missile (ABM) should not be interpreted as a threat. Eager to establish a lasting relationship, he was extraordinarily careful not to alarm them.

Threat can be an effective technique when one party has the power to inflict relatively large punishment on the other *without substantial retaliation*—and both parties know it. The strong party should not close its mind to the use of threat if long-run relationships and objectives are not violated. The critical question is whether the hostility generated is likely to result in an unstable agreement. There is little doubt in my mind that some negotiations are best settled by the use of threat. Much depends on situation and strategy.

A threat must be believed if it is to produce an agreement. President Truman could not figure out how to make the atom-bomb threat credible to the Japanese in World War II. They had never seen or heard of such a weapon and would probably have scoffed at the idea that a city could be destroyed by one bomb.

Threats can sometimes be made credible by escalation or consistency of behavior. Escalation builds credibility by exposing the opponent to small threats that are carried out, followed by larger threats if necessary. Most of us try to use the principle of consistency when we teach our children to expect punishment for irresponsible behavior. As any parent and Dean Rusk will testify, neither escalation nor consistency serves to make threat credible in all situations.

Size of threat is a major factor in its use. It was inappropriate to suggest use of nuclear weapons in response to the Pueblo hijacking. There is evidence that people block out massive threat, but are responsive to milder forms. The size of a threat must be scaled to the specific situation and its implication on long-run goals. I doubt if Hanoi would have believed General LeMay's threat to atom-bomb North Vietnam even if he had been elected Vice-President. It was completely out of proportion to the overall Vietnam problem.

Experiments indicate that threat is a tool of communication. When available, it is invariably used. These experiments show that when threat is used by both parties, they usually learn to get along better rather quickly. For years people will argue whether the 1969 Israeli blitz on Arab commercial planes was justified. One thing is certain: the Arabs know that retribution for sabotage will be swift and costly. Perhaps both parties will really negotiate in good faith when both have nuclear weapons and face mass destruction.

Threat is a dangerous technique because one may be forced to inflict greater punishment than issues warrant. I knew a man who threatened to throw his teenage daughter out of the house if she continued to use marijuana. To his regret (and perhaps hers), he threw her out and has yet to learn of her whereabouts. Recent research indicates that danger to both sides may be reduced if threat is implied rather than stated, mild rather than massive and rational rather than emotional. Strategy, with its focus on long-range goals, must be the guide governing its use.

HIDDEN LANGUAGE

People speak with and without words. Even when words are used, they often mean something other than what they say. On a nonverbal level, gestures and movements may tell a story that is as meaningful as words themselves.

Every society has its own way of doing things. E. T. Hall, a cultural anthropologist, in his book *The Silent Language* indicates that societies can be compared by looking at their attitudes toward sex, territory, time, space, learning, play and work.[28] For example, in some countries a man is not considered late if he keeps another waiting for an hour, whereas we Americans become uneasy after fifteen minutes. Hall points out that Arabs and Americans differ in their patterns of exchange. To an Arab, everything has a market value, and all intelligent people are supposed to be aware of what it is. If one party starts by offering very little, it is not for tactical reasons but rather an indication that he is ignorant of value. If a buyer begins by offering a little more than the ignorance price, it indicates that he wants to fight and argue but does not want to buy. A somewhat higher initial offer, one that is closer to the market price, signals that he is a bona fide buyer. If he starts by offering a price very close or at the pivotal market price, it indicates that he is eager to buy and will pay over the market. In our country many negotiators start from a low position in order to learn about their opponent's expectations. The low offer is considered tactically correct and is not associated with ignorance. Each demand and offer conveys a different message to the Arab than it does to the American.

Marshall McLuhan looks at hidden languages from the standpoint of media. He believes that every means of communcation has its own hypnotic language. Not only does he include radio, television and newspapers under the category of media, but also roads, comics, telephones, transportation, games and money. Each medium has its hidden assumptions. A book, for example, tends to imply that its author has knowledge based on diligent research. Furthermore, it implies that others, such as the publisher and bookseller, consider it worthwhile. A newscast on television or a report in the newspaper implies objectivity, which may or may not exist. Every media has a built-in language that only a few are aware of and most must search for if they wish to escape from its assumptions.

On an individual level, Freud was one of the first to emphasize the psychological importance of mannerisms and simple remarks in everyday affairs. S. S. Feldman, a psychiatrist, has made a lifelong study of this subject and developed his ideas in a book, *Mannerisms of Speech and Gestures in Everyday Life.*

Almost two hundred mannerisms, gestures and phrases are analyzed in his book. The hidden meaning of simple bodily movements such as face-rubbing, compressed lips, hands on temples, arms across chest, hand confusion and chain-smoking are discussed from a psychological standpoint. Phrases like "incidentally," "it's not terribly important," "to tell the truth," "I must admit," "of course," "in a way," and "before I forget" are seen by Dr. Feldman in terms of hidden meaning.

Sensitivity to nonverbal communication can hardly be developed by reading books alone. Rather it comes from observing people in their daily work and from wanting to know more about them.

DEADLOCK

The possibility of deadlock is one of the elements that lends excitement to negotiation. It is a technique that deserves to be well understood, but is not. Few experiments have explored the subject, although some of the work in psychological alienation does have relevance.

In our experiment a small number of people deadlocked. When I spoke to them afterward, they were intensely hostile to their opponents as well as to me for not providing more time and information with which to agree. I kept no statistics but could not help concluding that they were angry at themselves and would have much preferred an agreement.

Subsequently I engaged in a personal negotiation in which

my opponent and I had narrowed the settlement range to the point where agreement was imminent. I decided to try a small experiment in deadlock by deliberately creating an impasse. Two days later I called the opponent and agreed to his terms. Afterward I asked him how he had felt about the deadlock. He told me that he had suffered from shortness of breath, some loss of self-confidence, a degree of guilt and the fear that he would have to go through all this work again with somebody else. The strange thing was that I had created the situation but nevertheless suffered the same symptoms as he.

A sample of one can be misleading, but there is little doubt that deadlock is unpleasant. It is probably more intolerable to some people than to others, depending on their self-esteem and the alternatives available to them. In our experiment we found that people with high aspirations deadlock more than those whose aspirations are lower. However, high aspirants are more successful than others when they do not deadlock. There is reason to believe that deadlock, if used judiciously, can be an effective technique to win one's objectives.

PLACE OF NEGOTIATIONS

Where should a negotiation take place? At home if at all possible.

During a baseball season I did a statistical analysis of the outcome of the games played at home by all major-league teams. Of approximately 1,200 games completed by late July, 650 had been won and 550 lost at home. When we consider all the baseball clubs in both leagues, the probability of winning or losing a game at home is 50–50. The fact is that such a large number of victories could happen by accident less than one time in a hundred. In baseball a team definitely has a better chance at home than away. This finding is consistent with research reported by anthropologists and students of animal behavior, which indicates that there is a drive inherent in beast and man to set aside a homeland and protect it with unusual strength.

This does not mean that all negotiations can be conducted at home. If, however, a company has a choice, it should discuss important issues on its own premises. Where this is not possible the negotiating team should be provided ample comforts away from home to overcome natural disadvantages.

THE TECHNIQUE OF TIME

Timing maneuvers were considered earlier in this chapter. At that time we differentiated between a maneuver and a technique by pointing out that a maneuver was a general movement designed to secure a position of advantage while a technique was equivalent to a weapon or mechanism by which one can tune into a target. Time is a powerful weapon in the negotiator's arsenal of techniques.

Time is the common denominator by which various techniques can be integrated. Concessions can be combined with threats; moves with commitments; questions with caucus; informal discussions with trial balloons. There is a right time to commence negotiations and to introduce issues. Four o'clock on Friday afternoon of the last day of the month may be the best or worst of times, depending upon your position at the table.

The timing of a final commitment can contribute to its credibility. A commitment made early can look like a bluff, but a lesser final offer at two in the morning can be electrifying. Conversely, a caucus immediately after some insignificant point is raised can give that point disproportionate weight. A long-distance telephone call or a well-timed telegram can heighten the opponent's tension during the crisis phase. The replacement of a negotiator after a concession can be used as a signal that future concessions should not be expected.

Time talks.

CONCLUSION

Of the many maneuvers and techniques available, only a few have been covered in detail. For the most part the tactics suggested are theoretically sound and at the same time practical. Tactics are at best but tools of strategy. The undiscerning negotiator confuses one with another. The skilled planner knows the difference and therefore concentrates on strategy before he considers the details of maneuvers and techniques. These he selects with an eye toward the tactical mission— that is, to reduce the opponent's level of aspiration and probability of success while raising his satisfaction level.

CHAPTER 15

THE
SUCCESSFUL
MANAGER
NEGOTIATES

IT IS THE NEGOTIATING PROCESS WHICH CONSTITUTES THE
ACTIVITY PUTTING INTO PLAY THE PROCEDURES FOR
TAMING POWER. AT FIRST GLANCE, NEGOTIATION MAY
APPEAR TO BE AN INADEQUATE MEANS FOR SUCH AN
IMPORTANT TASK. NEVERTHELESS IT DOES EMBODY THE
DECISION-MAKING PROCEDURES WITHIN THE DAILY SCENE—
LEADING EVENTUALLY TO SOME KIND OF SETTLEMENT
SHORT OF THE USE OF RAW POWER.

Sylvia and Benjamen Selekman

How well we negotiate with superiors, associates and
subordinates has a *greater* effect on our lives than all the
buying and selling we will ever do. The idea of looking at
superior-subordinate relationships as a bargaining process is, at
first, strange. Those over forty grew up in an age when one
did not bargain with a boss but did as he was told. The world
has changed in the last twenty-five years. Today industry
speaks of participative management, collective decision-making

and shared responsibility at all levels, from assembly line to board room. The central activity of modern-day business is negotiation. In fact, one of Webster's definitions for negotiation is "to deal with or manage."

MODERN MANAGEMENT LOOKS AT THE WORKER

A new image of people at work has emerged that forever alters older concepts of management. Douglas McGregor, in his book *The Human Side of Enterprise*, defined the hidden assumptions of nineteenth-century management. Employers behaved as though people had an inherent dislike of work and sought to avoid it. On this basis they believed that men required control and coercion before they could be expected to produce.

McGregor had another theory. He believed that people want responsibility and are eager to do useful work once they understand its purpose. He believed that management should create opportunities for participation in decision-making and thereby release the productive potential inherent in people.

In 1938, more than twenty years before McGregor outlined his concept, another management theorist, Chester I. Barnard, wrote in *The Functions of the Executive* that the *authority of a superior was limited by what the subordinates would accept.* Barnard was a self-made man with little formal education who rose to a high position in the telephone industry. Based on a lifetime of experience he felt that the role of an executive was to coordinate information among executives, to plan and to secure the participation of subordinates in executing plans; whereas older management theorists had assumed that men worked for money and needed to be told precisely what to do, Barnard preferred to think of the worker in a higher sense. He believed that a man would contribute his efforts to a cause if a balance could be reached between his contributions and the inducements offered by management. Barnard was one of the first to recognize that nonmonetary inducements could be more effective than monetary rewards in securing participation. Although he did not describe the worker-manager relationship as a negotiation, the implication was clear that human beings engage in a bargaining process whenever they work together.

In this chapter we will describe six bargaining situations that involve executives in action on day-to-day problems. The situations are not fictitious, but names have been changed.

We will meet Tom, who made the mistake of taking the salary he was offered on the new job; Don and Bill, who are department managers with entirely different philosophies toward budgetary matters: Charlie, a superb program manager; Joe, who is competent but has trouble winning the respect of others; Harry, who has a gift for influencing people; and Jim, a man who goes from one missed deadline to another. Each of these men spends more time negotiating in their daily work than they ever will buying or selling.

NEGOTIATING SALARY ON THE NEW JOB

The biggest mistake Tom made was taking the job at the salary he did. He recognized the error a few weeks after coming to work, but it was too late. Five years later he has begun to recover the lost ground—at a cost of about $14,000. That's a lot of money for a middle-management executive to lose. What's worse, the loss could have been avoided.

Tom held a responsible position at one of the volatile conglomerates—you know, the kind that quickly builds up its force and then just as quickly wishes them a farewell. His turn came when his bosses' turn came. Because he had devotedly worked some fifty hours a week for six years, he was given special treatment, two weeks' notice instead of one.

Anyone who has ever earned $15,000 a year or more knows how hard it is to find a good job in two weeks.

Business was not bustling in California, and four weeks passed quickly. Despite the fact that Tom had fifteen years experience in purchasing and a college degree, he managed to obtain only three interviews. When one of these called back, he was as nervous as a kid getting a traffic ticket.

It was not a matter of money, but of pride. He had $5,000 in savings and his wife worked, so he could afford to wait; but the idea of doing so galled him. Besides, his father had been out of work during the depression and Tom remembered how hard it had been for him to find a job. When he reviewed his present situation he became frightened. His ability to get along with people, his thoughtful knowledge of purchasing and the fact that he had successfully risen to the rank of manager seemed trivial compared to getting through the interview.

The interview started amicably. The purchasing manager told him a great deal about the position and its long-run potential. He praised Tom's experience and expressed regret that the salary was 10 percent below his past earnings. He reassured him that although the title was assistant manager, the responsibilities were greater than on his previous job. In the course of the monologue, the interviewer mentioned how hard it was to get competent men. He had tried for eight weeks to fill the position and felt that Tom was the first man whose background and references were perfect. "Well," he said, "what do you think, Tom?" Tom grabbed it.

Four weeks later he was sorry. Aside from getting responses from several help-wanted ads he had answered, he learned through a computer run that his associates with equivalent responsibilities were earning 20 percent more. Furthermore, he had agreed to a salary at the bottom of the grade when the total range permitted almost a 30 percent spread. How could a man who had spent his entire business life negotiating with suppliers have agreed to a 10 percent cut without a murmur?

Easily. It was as though he had prepared himself for this event for a lifetime. The trouble was that he had a "little-shot" complex. Now, it isn't good to have a big-shot complex, but it's even worse to see yourself as less than you are. Instead of perceiving himself in terms of his achievements, his mind was preoccupied by how hard it had been to find work during the depression. Instead of raising his salary demands, he lowered them. Instead of looking for a director's or manager's job, he displayed a quick willingness to settle for less. Instead of listening and being perceptive to the interviewer's difficulties in finding a good manager, Tom dwelled on his own poor bargaining position. He did not pick up the message that the opponent had made up his mind and didn't want to go through the process any more than Tom did.

After a lifetime in business, Tom failed to realize that starting salary is negotiable. When asked what he wanted, he should have explained that in a few months he would have gotten a raise and was therefore looking for a 15 or 20 percent increase. He didn't do that, but rather meekly said that he wanted to meet his old salary. That initial demand was not high enough. When the interviewer's offer was made, Tom should have been willing to withstand the desire for closure and attempt to persuade him that more was necessary. Even had he failed in this, he might have extracted a promise for getting a 30-day hiring rate adjustment to restore parity; and other combinations, such as step-raises, and cost-of-living or bonus arrangements, could have been considered. None were.

Tom never looked at the matter as a negotiation. He failed to analyze the opponent's organizational and personal bargaining difficulties. He failed to build the joint-payoff by searching for solutions to mutual problems. He failed to analyze his own strategic objectives and tactics. He failed to recognize that power is always relative and that men applying for a job have more power than they think. It was a costly mistake.

BUDGET NEGOTIATIONS

In 1966, Governor Reagan announced that state agencies would be required to reduce manpower levels by 10 percent. There was an uproar as people (mostly Democrats) wondered how anybody could be insensitive to California's growing needs in education, welfare and mental health. In the aerospace industry we tend to take such cutbacks clamly because they are a way of life. We negotiate.

If our company president had announced a 10-percent cut in manpower, 10 percent of our people would have been laid off. However, Bill would have reduced his department by 12 percent and Don by only 8 percent. Bill is a consistent loser and Don a winner in budget negotiations.

Bill and Don are competent men who rose to responsible positions before they were thirty-five years old. They approach the annual budget by laying out objectives and determining manpower requirements. Both realize that objectives are never as clear-cut as they ought to be and that manpower allocations are, at best, only rough estimates. The difference between the two men in handling budget negotiations is worth understanding.

Bill does not believe that the budgetary process involves share bargaining but looks at it as a problem-solving session. After he makes a plan he reveals all facts to the director, including those areas in which uncertainty exists. If he is asked to cut back by ten men, he indicates as precisely as possible those activities that will be reduced and those that will remain adequately manned. The director has little trouble understanding Bill's presentation, as all areas are carefully delineated and open to inspection and adjustment.

Don uses a different approach. He tends to view the budgetary process as a negotiation in the broadest sense. While he recognizes that part of the process includes problem-solving, he never forgets that *share* bargaining exists. Don does not accept the idea that a 10-percent cut need affect him as it does others. He is also aware that his subordinates are likely to maintain a higher level of morale if the reduction is minimal.

From past experience he has learned that managers who can maintain hidden slack in their organization become available to do special jobs that the director needs done, but finds difficult to assign. Therefore Don pursues a negotiation policy that biases uncertainty in his favor and thereby overstates manpower requirements. He starts high and concedes slowly, as he would in a purchasing transaction. The results are pleasing. Don always has hidden slack in his organization. When business is bad he loses fewer men, and when business picks up, he gains manpower before his associates do.

Although both hold positions of equal responsibility at this time, some differences can be seen in the functioning of their departments. Don's people appear more relaxed, more informed and a bit more innovative than men in Bill's organization. When the director retires next year it's a toss-up as to whether Don or Bill will get the job. What do you think?

PROGRAM MANAGEMENT AND NEGOTIATION

The best program manager I ever met was Charlie. In the aerospace industry one learns to be a bit skeptical about people who promise to meet delivery dates and cost commitments. So rarely do such promises materialize that when they do one has to look for reasons to explain them. Charlie was indeed rare; he delivered what he promised.

The first program to which he was assigned was a small cost-plus-fixed-fee contract of $2 million. The problem was difficult: to design and produce a new computer display system in eighteen months on a tight budget. The manager of a small program normally has only two or three men working for him to keep track of changes and expenses. The actual design and manufacturing work is done by as many as fifteen different departments. The program manager is supposed to reach agreement with each department head in three vital areas: specification, delivery date and budget. He has complete responsibility for the program but no direct authority. When a program is large, the program manager has some power over the various engineering-design activities by virtue of size. The manager of a small program has little choice but to beg for a fair share of available engineering talent.

When department heads make promises of a financial or delivery nature they do so on the basis of assumptions regarding the performance of others on whom they depend. For example, the drafting room assumes that specifications will be released on a certain date and will change little thereafter. They then estimate the number of drawings and costs involved. If specifications are released late or unexpected changes occur, the drafting room is likely to overrun its commitment and miss its schedule. After years in the business, design managers believe in the domino theory: somebody in the process will fail before they do. Few take commitments with program managers very seriously. Charlie was different; he took engineering promises at face value and was not afraid of confrontation. He knew that the budgets and schedules that had been agreed to were tight but not unrealistic.

Engineering managers were the first to learn that Charlie expected them to live up to their word or explain why they had not. Government contracting officers also learned that agreements with him covering funding and engineering decisions had to be honored. Officials who failed to live up to their responsibilities without advising him promptly and giving a good explanation found themselves confronting Charlie in the boss's office. Invariably Charlie was prepared with facts and figures that the others never dreamed existed.

The division manager was delighted and supported him

against the influential department heads. Before long all were aware that Charlie negotiated a tough agreement but would live up to his end of the bargain. Consequently, negotiations became more serious and at the same time more realistic. Uncertainties were surfaced in a businesslike fashion.

Twenty-two months after the program began a computer display system was delivered at a cost of $2.2 million. This was an unheard-of performance record, a mere four-month delay and 10 percent overrun on a small but complex program.

Because he has shown the same competence on large engineering projects, Charlie has been promoted several times. I believe his success lies in an ability to negotiate effectively rather than in technical competence. He has an intuitive understanding of power and persuasion as well as a high level of aspiration. Today, as group executive, he continues to negotiate with the division managers reporting to him and with the company president to whom he reports.

WINNING RESPECT OF THE BOSS AND ASSOCIATES

Joe is forty and an accountant by profession. During his fifteen years in industry he has done an above-average job in a variety of functions and been rewarded with raises and promotions. However, despite above-average competence, Joe has never won the respect of his boss or associates. At this point in life he has learned to accept this failure.

Joe has a great many negotiation hangups, the worst of which are his defeatist attitude toward power and his low level of aspiration with regard to the respect due him as a person. At weekly staff meetings he always finds the seat closest to the manager. Nobody can remember when he last disagreed with the boss on any point, no matter how minor.

When a man resigns from Joe's staff, a crisis occurs. The thought of submitting a replacement requisition fills him with dread. He is like a man with a reasonable credit rating who won't go to the banker for fear the borrowing request will be denied. The manager senses Joe's apprehension but has budget problems of his own, so he allows him to stay understaffed. Joe, being a thoroughly insecure person, finds it necessary to work late every night in order to prove his loyalty and compensate for the lack of manpower.

The net result is a resounding shortage in Joe's *respect* account. Afraid of the chief's power and unsure of his own competence, Joe is willing to settle for little respect, and little is what he gets.

The subservient worker, no matter how *competent,* cannot negotiate respect from his superior or associates. To win respect one must act with dignity. Individuals who have a sense of identity and are involved with work for its own sake have respect for themselves. They are able to approach their bosses as equals. They recognize that each has something to give and something to get in the relationship. They accept authority but demand respect in return. The boss cannot help but reciprocate in this man-to-man negotiation.

MAKING FRIENDS AND INFLUENCING PEOPLE AT WORK

At 34, Harry is a millionaire. He deserves it not because he is a brilliant engineer but because of a unique ability to make friends and influence people at work, especially systems engineers.

Systems engineers are a difficult breed to work with. Like most creative people they occasionally come up with ideas that appear impractical. What makes it difficult is that "impractical" ideas are perceived to be quite practical by the designers. It requires a wise person to sift useful from useless concepts without alienating these talented people.

Harry is in charge of advanced-systems marketing for a

large company and has twenty of the most "way out" thinkers under him. They respect his judgment and intelligence. An active listener, he looks for hidden meanings in words and mannerisms. His response is rarely threatening to their status. Knowing the limits of power, he prefers to use persuasion rather than raw authority.

Harry spends most of his time negotiating with the men. Keenly aware of their achievement and status goals, he never permits himself or them to forget that company performance is the objective that makes personal aspirations possible.

When values conflicts arise in the engineering cost-control area, Harry negotiates an agreement. He does not hesitate to drive a hard bargain with the men and is not afraid to use power to win a critical point. Years ago he received stock options for this ability to reach workable and productive agreements with the "prima donnas" of the engineering profession. This special talent is not wasted when he confronts government officials in a marketing capacity. He is a great negotiator.

THE DEADLINE DILEMMA

Jim heads up the experimental machine shop in a large company but will soon be fired. He goes from deadline to deadline, breaks delivery promise after delivery promise.

Jim's customers are the design engineers, an elite group of creative people who seem to worry about time when they have run out of it. Most orders are brought to the shop with demands that they be completed the day after yesterday. The reasons for urgency are always good, but no better than the other 300 orders on the production board. Jim's problem is not intellectual; he is simply a poor negotiator—a man who can't say no.

In answer to the unreasonably high initial demands of the customer, Jim usually turns to production-control charts from which logical delivery dates are developed. The only trouble is, he assumes that all that can go wrong won't. Additionally, he fails to recognize that super-special requests from top management will, as they have in the past, continue to impose further demands on the already impossible schedule.

In short, the man responds to pressure by interpreting uncertainty factors in favor of the customer; he accepts the opponent's time constraints without similar understanding from them. The result is a promise that cannot be kept.

One would assume that Jim, having already been burnt, would learn. Unfortunately he is defensive in the face of power, for the engineers outrank him. "To fight with customers is wrong," he rationalizes. Unsure of his own merits and afraid of future consequences, he confuses confrontation with negotiation—and does neither.

If Jim could look at the engineers' requests as a negotiation, several alternatives would be evident. He would analyze power and recognize how important it is for engineers to get along with him. He would have statistics on hand that show shop realization to be less than perfect. He would prove that top management makes special requests that create havoc with the most reasonable priorities. He would counter the outrageous demands of the customer by offering equally outrageous promises. He would test the urgent needs of the engineer with all the facts, persuasion and authority at his command.

Unfortunately, Jim's inability to negotiate on the job never leaves enough time for his subordinates to do a job well. This and the deluge of late backorders will bring about his fall.

CONCLUSION

The critical element in management may well be the ability to formulate policy in such a way that a winning coalition can be mobilized behind it. For a man to do this effectively he must be aware of the subtleties and potentialities of power, persuasion, status, role and motivation. A winning coalition consists of men at various organizational levels, each with his own value system and goals. To reconcile these conflicting demands requires that the manager possess negotiating skills of a high order.

CHAPTER 16

LOVE,
HONOR
AND NEGOTIATE

THE SPECIFICATIONS OF MARRIAGE IMPOSE CHOICES. THE
PARTNERS CANNOT HAVE SEX RELATIONS AND NOT HAVE
THEM AT THE SAME TIME; THEY CANNOT GO TO THE PARTY
AND TO THE CONCERT TOGETHER AT THE SAME TIME;
THEY CANNOT REAR THE CHILDREN AS CATHOLIC AND AS
PROTESTANT; THEY CANNOT SPEND THE SAME MONEY FOR
SLIPCOVERS AND FOR THE POWER MOWER. SUCH ARE
AMONG THE KINDS OF DIFFERENCES WHICH CALL FOR AD-
JUSTMENTS.

Jessie Bernard

MARRIAGE IS LIKE LIFE—IT IS A FIELD OF BATTLE, AND
NOT A BED OF ROSES.

Virginibus Puerisque

At Esalen, a sensitivity training center in northern California,
a new approach to therapy is being tried. Ten married couples
join together for a weekend of confrontation. Each person is
asked to recall three dark secrets that they have never dared tell
their spouse. The marriage partners then make a public
confession of these thoughts. As you may suspect, a highly

charged emotional climate soon develops. The psychologists at Esalen believe that marriages are improved by the process. I do not agree.

My viewpoint is quite different. Whereas they believe in a full expression of innermost feelings, I believe that couples should adjust to each other by a negotiation process in which *tact, discretion and patience* play an important role. Conflict should be resolved by day-to-day bargaining and compromise rather than by dramatic confrontation.

Marriage is a negotiation that never ends. Married couples bargain at a conscious and subconscious level. Many who would not dream of openly manipulating the wants of their spouse do so by nonverbal gestures and mannerisms. The newly married husband quickly learns that a poorly prepared meal, dirty laundry and a slammed door have meaning.

Much has been written about the difference between husbands and wives. We can summarize by pointing out that some differences are a source of pleasure while others are not. Partners can get along even when they dislike their mate's taste in clothing, food or entertainment. However, there are differences that are so unpleasant and critical they can destroy a marriage.

The critical issues in marriage involve matters in which a choice in one direction precludes a choice in another. Newly married couples cannot have children early and not have them early; cannot invest substantial sums in apartment houses and enjoy expensive vacations. Among the major issues which tend to divide typical families are money, children, recreation, in-laws and sex. Whenever fundamental values of this nature are in conflict, marital adjustment takes place through negotiation.

What factors determine the outcome of marital conflict? In my opinion the same forces that determine the outcome of any negotiation govern marriage. Power and bargaining skill play as important a role here as they do in business. In a perfect world both partners would enjoy equality. Unfortunately they rarely do. Instead the marriage relationship tends to reflect the fundamental values and aspirations of the more skilled and powerful spouse.

One intriguing question that I have been asked is whether men are better negotiators than women. I believe they are. Men hold the trump cards in our society: financial power, planning skill, experience, status, competence, education and tradition. Women generally aspire to a subservient role in family decision-making and reap what they sow. There are, however, signs of change, indicating that women are coming up fast. Men, beware!

THE ELEMENTS OF MARRIAGE BARGAINING

Power is a key factor in marriage. Although tradition suggests that husbands hold the balance of power in decision-making, women are nibbling away at their prerogatives. A recent Detroit study indicates that the husband still enjoys more power where he contributes greater competence to the union.[27] Husbands who earn more money, work longer hours, possess good educations and hold prestige jobs tend to enjoy more power than those who do not.

The traditional power structure is under attack by American women as they flock to work in increasing numbers. The Detroit survey indicated that a wife's power grows in proportion to her financial contribution. The longer she works the more she takes over. In fact the takeover is complete where a man is unemployed and the woman works. The study also revealed that women have taken other roads to equal power— namely, through education and participation in outside affairs.

Division of labor and decision-making in the home contributes to the definition of objectives and thereby has its effect on marriage bargaining. Once more we find the employed wife on the march. It's getting harder to tell who does what in the home. Although men still do the handywork and women cook, there are important changes afoot. Men are doing more of the housework and shopping chores. Women are taking a larger role in financial management and bill-paying.

All is not lost, however. The Detroit study shows that female-dominated men are only henpecked to a degree: they quietly fight back by refusing to do as much work around the house as those men who enjoy equal power. Yes, it does appear that division of labor and decision-making in marriage are governed by the same forces as those in industry: ability, energy, tradition and knowledge.

When the study team investigated marital satisfaction, other elements of marriage negotiation came to light. They found that communication skill, social sense and aspiration level contributed to satisfaction.

The happiest wives were those who did not work but accepted the role of host-companion in their husband's business affairs. Those who were happy also reported that they discussed work problems with their spouse on a daily basis. The role of aspiration level was indeed interesting. Women who aspired to higher levels of companionship, sex, income, power and status tended to achieve higher goals and were happier than those who wanted less.

The negotiation game goes on from honeymoon through retirement. In this game one need not be a Morgan or a Vanderbilt to play, but skill is very important. The ability to negotiate effectively can be one factor that spells the difference between a tolerable and happy marriage. The people you are about to meet are "real." Several have done a poor job of bargaining and are paying a terrible price.

MONEY DIFFERENCES

Frank and Pearl have been married for twenty years and have two teenage children. He is proud of his competence as a certified public accountant and earns $25,000 a year. Frank is a happy husband, but Pearl is not a happy wife.

The problem is that he maintains full control of financial decisions and payment of bills. He has a simple method called the "box" system, and it works like this. As soon as the checking account reaches $1,000, Frank deposits a check in the savings account. When the savings account reaches $2,000 he deposits a check in the mutual-fund account. When the mutual-fund account reaches $5,000 he borrows on it and prepays the second mortgage on an apartment house they own. As a responsible person he also has a box for vacations, food, clothing and everything else. Unlike most of us he doesn't overrun his budget.

Pearl is aware that they are worth about $200,000. She also knows that the bank account is always short and that a fight can be precipitated by the purchase of a $30 dress or a few extra toll charges on the phone bill. She no longer enjoys "poor boy" summer holidays in Palm Springs, but can't seem to go anywhere else because it really is a good deal in July when the temperature reaches 110°.

Pearl is beginning to suspect that she has negotiated herself into the biggest box of all. Having no strategy of her own, she became a victim of her husband's financial plans and aspirations. He held the balance of power by virtue of superior planning, hard work, determination and knowledge. Even when she tried to suggest years ago that they move into a better house, he countered by proving that they could hardly afford to liquidate certain assets. It was simply too difficult and unpleasant to argue or find out about these complex matters.

Today it's too late. Frank knows that Pearl no longer enjoys listening to his tax-deduction triumphs. His level of aspiration for a reasonably good life is low while his desire for capital is high. Pearl has given up. She no longer has enough power, skill or determination to change the pattern or get divorced. I suspect that their children will someday have a lot of fun with the money.

A TEENAGE DILEMMA

Bruce is sixteen and lives in a well-to-do area in Los Angeles. He attends a private school, has a nice room, a stereo and his own car. The truth is that he is a budding monster—not a very nice kid.

The trouble may have started years ago when his parents capitulated to his childish whims. When he refused to clean his room or keep his clothes neat, the maid took over these responsibilities. Instead of an allowance he was given whatever he said he needed. His work in school is not taken too seriously because his parents feel he will undertake a business career in his early twenties. He, on the other hand, hopes to find his true profession at age thirty and has absolutely no idea of what it will be. Bruce is having a marvelous time. He smokes "pot," takes LSD, stays out until three in the morning and hangs around with a group of wild but well-heeled kids in the neighborhood.

Recently things got so bad at home that he was thrown out of the house. His father hoped that a taste of the "hard life" would provide therapy. It did not. On the contrary, Bruce moved into a $50-a-month Hollywood "pad" with three other "cop-outs." He had no trouble absorbing the 42¢-a-day overhead charge out of his savings. It was the first taste of the real joys of life: good companionship and freedom from responsibility.

After a month in these idyllic surroundings his distraught mother arranged a summit conference at a local pizza parlor. The boy registered demands that included complete amnesty, a better car, pot-smoking privileges at home, his own apartment during the summer and field trips to Berkeley during times of "action."

Bruce knew how to exploit power. He properly sensed his mother's anxiety and recognized that it would be difficult for his father to enforce the banishment. He learned quickly that in family negotiations it is the person most committed to a relationship who gives up power. The boy had successfully converted "no power" into bargaining strength.

As of this writing he is home, having won most of the issues. In a few years Bruce will enter a university and confront the president with a carefully prepared list of non-negotiable demands. He shows great promise for this type of work, having won easy victories at home.

IN-LAWS

Jules and Kathy had a terrible courtship. He is Jewish and she Catholic. Jules began the most difficult negotiation of his life the day his Orthodox parents learned that he wished to marry.

From that moment on he found himself discussing the issues with aunts and uncles, cousins and neighbors. The family decided that there was only one honorable way out: Kathy was to become Jewish. Young and eager to please his elders, Jules confronted her with the family proposal.

Kathy refused to go along with the plans but did concede to visit a local rabbi for a quick "noncredit" course in Judaism. As the wedding deadline approached, nothing was settled. The family decided that a commitment would settle matters once and for all. They made a public announcement that Jules would be considered dead if he proceeded with the civil ceremony without converting Kathy. The commitment backfired when the couple eloped. It would be nice to say that they enjoyed a wonderful honeymoon, but in fact it was miserable because both were distraught.

About a month after returning, Jules arranged for Kathy to meet his family for the first time. The parents prepared a nice spread and were surprisingly gracious. Neighbors found excuses to borrow an egg so they could see the strange bride. Instead of abusing Kathy as Jules had feared, the parents fooled him. They spent two hours telling her what a weak-spined, unreliable person she had married. By this time, Kathy was reasonably sure they were correct. Had they told her prior to the wedding, it might never have occurred. However, the negotiation continued for another year and pressure was put upon her to convert. One evening she made a commitment. Either Jules was to forget about the conversion or she would forget about him. It worked. They are still together, and surprisingly happy.

S E X

One hundred years ago a good sexual adjustment was one in which the husband was considerate and the wife submissive. With the turn of the century women were emancipated, making life more difficult for men. Women raised their sexual aspirations and even had the audacity to blame lack of fulfillment on their mates. Higher aspirations soon brought them greater satisfaction.

Sexual adjustment today results from a bargaining process between partners whose tastes, demands and limits differ. We will not dwell on differences but rather on elements of the negotiation itself. All the factors are there: power, exchange, satisfaction, persuasion, communication and division of labor.

The communication of sex may be verbal or nonverbal, hidden or overt. Most men have heard and understand such phrases as "I'm tired," "There's a good TV movie on" or "The children are awake." On a nonverbal level they have learned to read special meaning into a wink, a sigh, a winsome smile or what have you.

Power plays a role in sex. Few would deny that such sources of power as reward, punishment, legitimacy (tradition), knowledge, commitment (love), competition, time and effort play a part in sexual adjustment. Each partner exerts a degree of strength over the other and learns to accommodate to the balance of power.

The anatomy of bargaining certainly applies to sexual adjustment. Sex involves joint problem-solving, attitude-structuring, in-group bargaining, personal bargaining, and a rationing process.

Sex can be thought of in terms of exchange. We know there are women who trade sex for security and men who exchange freedom of choice for stability. In a successful marriage both partners gain satisfaction. If on the other hand the relationship offers too little to one or both, deadlock follows. In the marketplace of sex, a frigid wife or unresponsive husband soon learns that alternate sources of supply exist.

CONCLUSION

This is not a book about marriage. There is, however, good reason to view marriage in a negotiation context. Successful marriage negotiation resembles mature collective bargaining more than it does the Paris peace talks. This is because the problem-solving process in an old and valued relationship takes precedence over share bargaining.

With respect to the techniques suggested at Esalen, it appears to me that the exchange of deep dark secrets makes as little sense in the world of marriage as it does in business. Tact, patience, timeliness, commitment, empathy and persuasion are better means to marital adjustment than is confrontation.

It would be nice to think that our divorce rate would go down if the marriage vow were changed to read, "love, honor and negotiate."

CHAPTER 17

ORGANIZE
TO WIN YOUR
OBJECTIVES

RESOURCES, TO PRODUCE RESULTS, MUST BE ALLOCATED
TO OPPORTUNITIES RATHER THAN PROBLEMS.

Peter Drucker

THE PROCESS IS THE PRODUCT.

Nino Zappala

There is a story about negotiation that I have heard repeated time and again by businessmen. It seems that J. P.
Morgan, the legendary financier, met Cornelius Vanderbilt,
the richest man in the world, on a luxury liner crossing the
Atlantic. As they sat on adjoining deck chairs Vanderbilt
intimated that he was interested in disposing of iron properties
in Michigan. Morgan, having already acquired steelmills, was
anxious to develop raw-material sources. According to the
story, Morgan made an offer of $60 million, which was im-
mediately accepted. One of the biggest transactions of the nine-
teenth century was settled in an instant.

Morgan chuckled when he told others about the deal, for
he had been prepared to pay $80 million. Vanderbilt also loved

to tell the story because he was convinced that the great financier had outfoxed himself. Vanderbilt's price would have been
$40 million.

With due respect to their business wisdom, in this instance
both were poor negotiators. That they expressed satisfaction
with the outcome is not unusual. Knowledge about negotiation has progressed little since J. P. Morgan's day. Businessmen
are as unaware now as they were then that performance can
be improved if they organize to win. Yet, the stakes are high.
I have seen managers push, threaten and plead with their
employees to meet tight production budgets which were tight
only because the manager himself made bad mistakes at the
bargaining table. With proper training and organization, such
mistakes can be avoided.

The program to be proposed is practical. It can be implemented at relatively low cost and with a minimum of organizational disruption. All that is required is a commitment to
improve performance and a recognition that modern concepts
are necessary.

A POSITIVE, TOUGH-MINDED PROGRAM

There are four parts to the program. Phase I and II
should be implemented together. Phase III and IV involve
organizational rethinking and may be initiated later. For best
results the entire proposal should be adopted. If this is not
possible, substantial gains can still be realized by partial
implementation. The four phases of the program are:

    I. Improve negotiation planning
   II. Establish a broad-based training program
  III. Improve the negotiator selection process
  IV. Establish a high-level negotiation activity

This program rests on the premise that a company or

nation should negotiate to win its objectives and not be content with place or show. It cannot do so without superior organization and planning.

PHASE I — IMPROVE NEGOTIATION PLANNING

Over 90 percent of the businessmen in our survey ranked planning the most important trait. In my opinion it is typically a weak area. The following steps must be taken to assure that planning is effective.

1. Ask probing questions about power, objectives, aspiration level and other factors in this book.

2. Improve information gathering and assumption testing processes.

3. Understand the difference between strategic, administrative and tactical planning and see that each is done in the proper organizational climate and order.

4. Perform high-quality worth-analyses.

5. Develop an understanding of the wide range of tactical maneuvers and techniques available.

6. Understand the anatomy of negotiation and its applicability.

7. Inoculate for success.

8. Organize people and resources for maximum impact at the table.

To implement this part of the program two decisions are necessary. First, management must raise its aspirations with respect to what it considers good planning. Second, it must learn more about planning so it can better understand the difference between the good and the mediocre. Until management makes these two decisions, planning is apt to be superficial.

PHASE II—A BROAD-BASED TRAINING PROGRAM

Negotiation training is a high-return business investment. It takes but a single success at the bargaining table to more than recover the entire cost of training a man. There is probably no other activity in which improved skill can so quickly be converted to profit.

In discussing the matter of techniques with training specialists I find that there are two approaches. One tends to be heavily how-to-do oriented while the other is how-to-think or concept oriented. A course in negotiation must be a blend of both. Meaningful training cannot avoid dealing in concepts. Men will get little out of a how-to-do program unless they are provided with a frame of reference that permits them to interpret past experience and think for themselves when unforeseen problems arise. There is no reason why the idea of teaching concepts to practical negotiators should frighten any training people. Concepts are simply ways of looking at reality. They can be explained in common-sense terms and illustrated by every-day example. Yet the idea of teaching concepts to practical negotiators frightens some training people. It need not.

The curriculum should also acquaint the men with recent research findings in the field. Computer centers and laboratories throughout the country are developing new information at an increasing rate. If the material is carefully sifted and understood by the instructor, it can prove exciting and useful.

No course in negotiation would be complete without a thorough consideration of the realities of strategy and tactics.

It is here that the advantage of a logical framework will best permit the negotiator to integrate theory with practice in a usable way.

What is the best way to teach such a course? I have little doubt that a lecture approach is the *least* effective. It is too easy on the students and instructor. In my experience the best method is the roundtable seminar, in which discussion of basic concepts and principles is encouraged under strong, knowledgeable leadership. Active involvement and commitment on the part of those who teach and those who learn will make both more responsible.

The value of seminar discussions can be enhanced by mock bargaining sessions designed to illustrate sound principles. I have attended classes in which days were spent dickering for make-believe widgets without ever coming to grips with a single substantial idea. Admittedly the men enjoyed such relaxation, but it taught them little. I would rather see the time spent on short cases that permit small group interaction on issues related to basic building blocks like power or decision-making.

Because paid learning is never inexpensive it is necessary to determine how best to use a limited training budget. In keeping with the idea that a company should concentrate its resources on opportunities, I suggest that training begin with top executives and program managers. It takes but a few hours for a high-level corporate executive or program manager to earn or lose millions at the bargaining table.

The training program should include personnel from sales, purchasing and contracts as well as a limited number of design engineers. It would be short-sighted to exclude senior engineers, who regularly provide technical assistance at the bargaining table. The full impact of a training investment can best be realized if all members of the negotiation team know what they are doing and why.

PHASE III—IMPROVING THE SELECTION PROCESS

Just because a man engages in negotiation in the course of his work is of itself no reason to believe that he negotiates well. An excellent salesman or lawyer may be a mediocre negotiator.

When products were less complex and three-bid buying more prevalent, it was no great risk to assume that competent buyers were likely to be good bargainers. Today, the Department of Defense procures 90 percent of its requirements on a negotiated basis. The percentage is not as high in commercial concerns but continues to rise every year. In view of the growing stakes it is time we focused on the selection process.

A price-support specialist attends twenty or thirty major negotiations a year. He is thereby able to observe the abilities of a large number of men during the planning and implementation phases of the process. As such an observer, I was surprised that negotiating skill could vary so greatly. Later, when conducting experiments with this variable, I found that skilled men did indeed outperform unskilled men by a wide margin when both possessed roughly equal power.

Throughout the research that went into this book it was clear that personality factors contribute dramatically to effective bargaining. It therefore makes sense to select men carefully by taking the following steps:

1. The selection of representatives should be based upon *disciplined* observation. Opinions of managers should be supplemented by the opinions of trained observers, who evaluate the men in action.

2. Psychological tests should be given those responsible for high-dollar-value transactions. Men with serious problems associated with self-esteem, power and ambiguity should not represent the company.

Improved selection and training go together. Unless managers and observers know what to look for, they have less chance to find the competent man they seek.

PHASE IV — NEGOTIATION, A TOP-LEVEL FUNCTION

Each year there are only a few negotiations *essential* to the well-being of a firm. In a small company the owner handles these, for his business is at stake. In large corporations the criteria for selection are usually based on the fact that a man is a good administrator, engineer or lawyer. In neither the large nor small company is the chief negotiator selected on his proven ability as a professional negotiator.

In my opinion most firms would benefit by organizing a small but elite group of negotiators who would report to the company president and would be responsible for providing the services outlined below.

1. Conduct all *essential* corporate negotiations regardless of whether they involve sales, purchasing, rate regulations, labor, acquisitions or contract termination. Although I recognize that members of the elite group cannot be specialists in all things, I am assuming that they are extraordinarily motivated and intelligent and therefore able to get to the heart of issues efficiently. From time to time it may be necessary to assign them to problems of such complexity as to require years of preparation. I have participated in multimillion-dollar negotiations that were two years in the making.

2. Provide consulting services to line organizations at preproposal, proposal and preconference stages on negotiations of lesser magnitude.

3. *Create a negotiation climate* among procurement, contracting, sales and engineering personnel.

4. Provide *assistance* in the selection of competent negotiators at all company levels.

5. Act in the role of Devil's Advocate under special circumstances.

6. Establish a formal *internship* program for improving the skill of *special candidates.*

Except for the internship program the responsibilities are self-explanatory. It is well known that the training of medical doctors is not complete until they serve an internship program under the direction of senior professors. There is no reason why the practice should not be adapted to the development of a limited number of carefully selected negotiators.

Interns would have a unique opportunity to develop a conceptual understanding of their profession and to watch principles put into action by senior men who know what they are doing and can describe their actions in a disciplined manner. Training of this scope is not as expensive as it may appear, for interns can perform many necessary duties for senior representatives while they learn. If candidates are screened by a broad-based team including a top executive, a psychologist, a psychiatrist and the chief of the elite group they are likely to learn much from the internship program and emerge as truly essential members of the firm.

It would be short-sighted to select and train members of the elite group so intensively and not reward them with money, status and security. Unless provided with high salaries, stock options and job tenure it is likely that they will be lost to other companies.

The argument for an elite cadre of negotiators is very strong, but its implementation will require courage on the part of management. They face a difficult choice. On the one hand they can continue to use ordinary lawyers and contract specialists to negotiate essential contracts and none will be the wiser. On the other hand they can recognize and organize negotiation as a specialized profession requiring training, knowledge and intelligence of the highest order. The latter choice is difficult but far-sighted. It allocates the best resources where the greatest opportunities are to be found.

MEASURING RESULTS

We must now face a difficult problem. As executives we would like to know whether our negotiator performed well. Except on rare occasions, I do not believe that we will ever be able to measure the outcome of a negotiation in relation to what might have been.

I would rather see us spend our energy measuring the process rather than the product. If we really plan well, select our people carefully, train them in a sophisticated rather than dilettante fashion and organize to use our very best men, we cannot help but do well over the long haul.

This does not mean that we will never do poorly, for there are many factors that determine outcome, not the least of which is the relative skill and power of the opponent. What is important is the overall balance of professionalism in negotiation wherein those who are most systematic and knowledgeable do better than those who rely on intuition alone. It is the force of probability that favors the former.

The best thing about measuring the process and not the negotiator is that the one can be done and the other cannot. We can aspire to the best planning, best selection, best training and best organization possible within our resources. It is much simpler to recognize the best than to discern minute differences between the good and the mediocre. The best cries out, "If this is not the finest, what is?" The mediocre and "good enough" cannot ask such a question.

Negotiation involves so much of value that only an investment in the finest will provide the largest return for the lowest cost. Measure the process and the product is likely to turn out well.

CONCLUSION

Every significant negotiation contains a "zone of not knowing" where risk is difficult to assess and reality blurred. A skilled man can change the outcome by as much as 5 or 10 percent. For a large firm this may mean tens of millions of profit dollars. For the government the opportunities are even greater. These gains can be realized by organizing to win.

CHAPTER 18

THE
WHEEL OF
NEGOTIATION

A WISE MAN WILL MAKE MORE OPPORTUNITIES THAN
HE FINDS.

Sir Francis Bacon

INHERENTLY, EVERY PROBLEM IS IN SOME WAY AN
OPPORTUNITY.

Jack Karrass

THE FAULT, DEAR BRUTUS, IS NOT IN OUR STARS,
BUT IN OURSELVES, THAT WE ARE UNDERLINGS.

William Shakespeare

The important negotiation decisions today are being made
by men employed by the organizations they represent. Not long
ago it was the entrepreneur who did his own bargaining because he personally profited by doing the job well. The
organization man is not motivated by the same goal; he will be
paid a salary whether the outcome is mediocre or excellent. All
he need do is offer a reasonable explanation of the results.
When the organization man does respond energetically to the

challenge of negotiation, it is usually not because of personal profit but from a desire to achieve and excel in a difficult game. Not all men respond in this way, for the selection process of larger organizations tends to favor those with bureaucratic rather than entrepreneural tendencies. All too often the criterion for a good deal is one that does not "rock the boat."

There are deeper reasons why men do not negotiate with the determination they once did. Western society is rapidly changing from one of survival-orientation to one of affluence for all. Just a few years ago we lived in a world where being a good bargainer was important because it meant the difference between eating and going hungry. One has only to watch two Mexican peasants bargain for a $10 serape to see how seriously they take the process. In our country we have less need to drive a hard bargain.

For those of us in business these changes can prove to be an opportunity or a problem, for, in some ways, every problem is an opportunity. If businessmen can create an entrepreneural climate of negotiation and select achievement-oriented representatives who have high aspirations and know how to negotiate, the opportunities for gain are good. For those who continue to negotiate in time-honored ways, losses are inevitable.

Systematic research in this field is barely in its infancy, but it is already apparent that better ways are emerging. For those who are willing to recognize that new understanding is necessary the future will be bright.

THE WHEEL

The key to winning objectives lies in knowing how to negotiate more effectively. This is true whether the exchange concerns buying or selling, law or diplomacy, marriage or management; the elements of success are the same.

The Wheel of Negotiation was deliberately so drawn. Men

may reach their goals afoot but the journey will be long and full of risk. (Indeed, for some who negotiate, the wheel is yet to be invented.) The wheel provides a better way.

Our wheel has seven spokes composed of the basic elements of negotiation. These elements may be constructed of strong steel or termite-ridden wood. The wheel itself may still function even if most of its spokes are missing or defective. But how dependably?

Similar to the automobile tire, the rim is made of fibers—fibers consisting of planning, strategy, techniques and a few lesser-known materials. To continue our analogy, automobiles once ran reasonably well on welded steel hoops. This was satisfactory until somebody designed the solid-rubber tire. Though

THE WHEEL OF NEGOTIATION

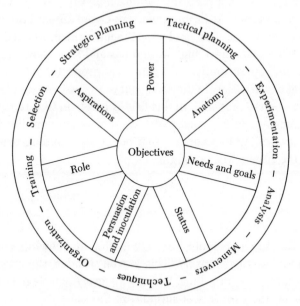

Figure 10. THE WHEEL OF NEGOTIATION

it is possible to ride long distances on bald or defective or outdated tires, no one would enter the Indianapolis "500," or any lesser race, on recaps and expect to win.

So it is with the negotiation wheel. Developments have evolved that make it possible to improve its basic structure and dependability. The key issue, then, is the amount of risk today's executive is willing to take. The forward-looking executive will not tolerate the unnecessary risk inherent in a defective or out-moded wheel, especially when the stakes are high and the bargaining pressures heavy. He will insist on utilizing a strong negotiation structure; one that will safeguard his objectives and assure that they are reached. This is the only sound insurance policy to protect his interests at the bargaining table.

THE EMERGING PROFESSION

Negotiation is an emerging profession. The "era of negotiation" President Nixon spoke of only a short while ago is upon us. College administrators can no longer prescribe curriculum from wood-paneled offices, and the story in our high schools is much the same. Workers in the public sector will never again accept the dictates of a city council that denies their right to bargain collectively.

There is a revolution going on in the work world that merits our attention. The autocratic boss is on his way out. Men are beginning to search for identity by demanding a part in decision-making. Within the next few years black people will demand and get a larger role in management. These assaults will be mild compared with the confrontation certain to come between Negroes and those craft unions that have not tried hard to provide openings. When these forces collide, higher management will be caught in the middle, for they will either settle the disputes or watch profits go up in smoke or idleness.

The revolution of rising expectations will be heard in the

home. Already the structure of traditional authority is being tested to its limit. The dominance of husband over wife, parent over child, old over young, is under fire. None will accept second-class citizenship in the home. Family members no longer have an economic need for one another. Parents of teen-agers are beginning to suspect this. The kids already know it.

The choice is between negotiating with one another or destroying our institutions. I have confidence that we will succeed in working out our problems because we have had practice in bargaining by virtue of our democratic institutions. One day, not many years from now, the young from totalitarian and tradition-bound countries will be affluent enough to rise in protest. Their upheavals will make ours appear like child's play because they are less experienced in the exchange of ideas. Yes, the "era of negotiation" is upon us—with a vengeance born of affluence.

To resolve the business and social conflicts of society, each of us will have to become better negotiators. This means that we will have to know more about the process and its basic elements. For those who negotiate in their daily work the problem is more acute. Once some companies begin to treat negotiation as a profession, all companies will have to follow. When selected men are provided specialized knowledge and a long period of intensive preparation, they will be very hard to match at the bargaining table. These professionals will have high aspirations and know how to negotiate to win their objectives. They will be prepared to participate effectively in the negotiating society.

NOTES

In the course of research one discovers an amazing abundance of useful material. It is possible to give credit to but a few of the men and women who stimulated my interest in this subject. For the reader who desires a larger bibliography, I suggest that he refer to my dissertation on file at the University of Southern California, Los Angeles.

1. WILLIAM L. SHIRER, *The Rise and Fall of the Third Reich.* New York: Simon & Shuster, 1959.
2. *Newsweek*, December 2, 1968.
3. HAROLD NICOLSON, Diplomacy, 3d ed. revised. London: Oxford University Press, 1963.
4. GERALD H. SHURE and ROBERT J. MEEKER, "A Personality/Attitudinal Schedule for Use in Experimental Bargaining Studies," *Journal of Psychology*, March 1967.
5. SIDNEY SIEGEL and LAWRENCE E. FOURAKER, *Bargaining and Group Decision Making*, New York: McGraw-Hill Book Co., 1960.
6. KURT LEWIN *et al.*, "Level of Aspiration," *Personality and Behavior Disorders*, J. McV. Hunt, ed. New York: Ronald Press Co., 1944.
7. DAVID C. MCCLELLAND, *The Achieving Society.* New Jersey: D. Van Nostrand Company, Inc., 1961.
8. THOMAS C. SCHELLING, *The Strategy of Conflict.* Cambridge: Harvard University Press, 1960.
9. JOHN W. ATKINSON and NORMAN T. FEATHER, *A Theory of Achievement Motivation.* New York: John Wiley & Sons, Inc., 1966.

10. SEYMOUR L. ZELEN, *Effects of Frustration and Level of Adjustment Upon the Reality of Goal Attainment Methods.* Unpublished Ph.D. dissertation. University of California, Los Angeles, 1963.
11. DORWIN CARTWRIGHT (ed.), *Studies in Social Power.* Ann Arbor: University of Michigan, Institute for Social Research, 1959.
12. CARL I. HOVLAND and IRVING L. JANIS, *Personality and Persuasibility,* New Haven: Yale University Press, 1959.
13. CARL I. HOVLAND *et al., Order of Presentation in Persuasion.* New Haven: Yale University Press, 1957.
14. *Ibid.*
15. LINTON and GRAHAM, Chapter 4, "Personality Correlates of Persuasion," *Personality and Persuasibility.* New Haven: Yale University Press, 1959.
16. SIR FRANCIS BACON, *The Essays of Francis Bacon,* "Of Negotiating," 225-227, ed. Mary Augusta Scott. New York: Charles Scribner's Sons, 1908.
17. WILLIAM J. MCGUIRE, "Resistance Against Persuasion," *Journal of Abnormal and Social Psychology,* April 1962.
18. THORSTEIN VEBLEN, *The Theory of the Leisure Class.* New York: The Macmillan Co., 1899.
19. DANIEL KATZ and ROBERT L. KAHN, *The Social Psychology of Organizations.* New York: John Wiley & Sons, Inc., 1966.
20. ABRAHAM H. MASLOW, *Motivation and Personality.* New York: Harper and Brothers, 1954.
21. WILLIAM F. WHYTE, *Money and Motivation.* New York: Harper & Row, Publishers, 1955.
22. FREDERICK HERZBERG, *Work and the Nature of Man.* Cleveland: The World Publishing Company, 1966.
23. RICHARD E. WALTON and ROBERT B. MCKERSIE, *A Behavioral Theory of Labor Negotiations.* New York: McGraw-Hill Book Co., 1965.
24. This note refers to various experiments by Morton Deutsch, Gerald H. Shure, Leonard Solomon and Douglas P. Crowne, each of which indicates that "nice guys don't win by being nice" if their opponents persist in being competitive.
25. ANN DOUGLAS, *Industrial Peacemaking.* New York: Columbia University Press, 1962.
26. C. TURNER JOY, *How Communists Negotiate.* New York: Macmillan Co., 1955.
27. ROBERT O. BLOOD and DONALD M. WOLFE, Husbands and Wives. Glencoe, Ill.: Free Press, 1960.
28. EDWARD T. HALL, *The Silent Language.* New York: Fawcett World Library, 1959.

ACKNOWLEDGMENTS

Serious work on a subject as complex as negotiation cannot be accomplished without help. I wish to acknowledge the far-sighted research support provided by the Hughes Aircraft Company and its executives. While all of them were helpful, Theodore Kotsovolos and William A. Van Allen were particularly so. Both had the wisdom to know the difference between a cost and an investment.

Appendix I
COMPARISON OF TRAIT RANKINGS
(Professional Commercial Negotiators)

	BUYING MGRS.	BUYERS	CONTRACT MGRS.	SUPPLIER REPR.	DESIGN ENGRS.	PROGRAM MGRS.
Task-Performance Group						
Stamina	7	7	7	7	7	7
Planning	1	1	1	1	1	1
Product knowledge	5	4	4	2	3	4
Reliability	6	6	6	5	6	6
Goal-striving	2	5	3	3	4	2
Problem-solving	3	3	5	6	5	5
Initiative	4	2	2	4	2	3
Aggression Group						
Persistence	4	3	2	1	3	4
Risk-taking	5	5	6	6	6	3
Power-exploitation	1	2	3	2	2	1
Competitiveness	3	4	4	3	4	5
Defensiveness	7	7	7	7	7	7
Courage	6	6	5	5	5	6
Team leadership	2	1	1	4	1	2
Social Group						
Trust	8	7	6	6	8	7
Patience	5	4	4	4	4	4
Personal attractiveness	4	5	5	5	5	5
Personal integrity	1	1	1	1	2	2
Tact	2	2	2	3	1	1
Open-mindedness	3	3	3	2	3	3
Appearance	6	6	7	7	6	8
Compromising	7	8	8	8	7	6

Appendix I (Continued)

	BUYING MGRS.	BUYERS	CONTRACT MGRS.	SUPPLIER REPR.	DESIGN ENGRS.	PROGRAM MGRS.
Communication Group						
Verbal clarity	1	1	1	1	1	1
Warm rapport	4	4	5	3	4	6
Listening	2	2	2	2	3	3
Nonverbal	7	7	7	7	7	7
Debating	5	5	3	5	5	4
Coordinating	3	3	4	4	2	2
Role-playing	6	6	6	6	6	5
Self-Worth Group						
Gain opponent's respect	1	1	1	2	1	2
Self-esteem	2	2	4	4	3	1
Personal dignity	6	5	2	3	6	5
Gain boss's respect	5	7	7	6	7	7
Ethical standard	3	3	3	1	4	6
Organizational rank	8	8	8	8	8	8
Self-control	4	4	5	5	2	4
Risk being disliked	7	6	6	7	5	3
Thought Group						
Negotiating experience	6	5	6	7	6	4
General practical intelligence	2	1	2	1	2	2
Broad perspective	7	7	7	5	3	7
Insight	4	6	4	3	7	5
Decisiveness	5	4	3	6	5	3
Analytical ability	3	3	5	4	4	6
Clear thinking under stress	1	2	1	2	1	1
Education	8	8	8	8	8	8

Appendix II
COMPARISON OF TRAIT RANKINGS
(Professional Commerical Negotiators)

	ATTORNEYS	ACCOUNTANTS	RETAIL-CLOTHING BUYERS	REAL-ESTATE SALESMEN
Task-Performance Group				
Stamina	7	7	7	7
Planning	1	1	1	4
Product knowledge	3	4	3	3
Reliability	5	5	6	5
Goal-striving	6	6	2	1
Problem-solving	2	2	5	6
Initiative	4	3	4	2
Aggression Group				
Persistence	2	2	2	2
Risk-taking	6	6	4	1
Power-exploitation	1	1	3	4
Competitiveness	4	3	5	3
Defensiveness	7	7	7	7
Courage	5	5	6	5
Team leadership	3	4	1	6
Social Group				
Trust	6	7	7	8
Patience	4	5	6	3
Personal attractiveness	5	4	4	6
Personal integrity	1	1	1	1
Tact	3	2	3	2
Open-mindedness	2	3	2	4
Appearance	8	6	5	5
Compromising	7	8	8	7
Communication Group				
Verbal clarity	1	1	1	1
Warm rapport	3	3	4	3
Listening	2	2	2	2
Nonverbal	7	7	7	7
Debating	5	6	5	6
Coordinating	4	4	3	5
Role-playing	6	5	6	4
Self-Worth Group				
Gain opponent's respect	1	3	2	2
Self-esteem	2	1	1	1
Personal dignity	5	4	4	5
Gain boss's respect	7	7	7	7
Ethical standard	4	2	3	3
Organizational rank	8	8	8	8
Self-control	3	5	5	4
Risk being disliked	6	6	6	6

Appendix II (Continued)

	ATTORNEYS	ACCOUNTANTS	RETAIL-CLOTHING BUYERS	REAL-ESTATE SALESMEN
Thought Group				
Negotiating experience	6	7	7	7
General practical intelligence	4	3	2	2
Broad perspective	7	4	5	4
Insight	3	5	6	6
Decisiveness	5	6	4	5
Analytical ability	2	2	1	3
Clear thinking under stress	1	1	3	1
Education	8	8	8	8

ABOUT THE AUTHOR

DR. CHESTER L. KARRASS was recipient of the first Howard Hughes Doctoral Fellowship in Business Administration at the age of 42. After twenty years of industrial experience in high-dollar-value negotiations, he was provided the opportunity to do what many seasoned executives would like to do—that is, to devote three years to full-time study in the areas of modern decision theory, quantitative methods, finance and marketing. This book has grown out of that study and is designed to synthesize a lifetime of negotiating experience with today's advanced ideas in the economic and social sciences.

Dr. Karrass is a Negotiation Consultant for Hughes Aircraft Company and other major corporations. He conducts seminars on the subject for professionals and executives. When not writing or doing research, he enjoys speaking to management clubs and professional organizations.

He is an engineering graduate with a master's degree from Columbia University and a doctorate from the University of Southern California.

With his wife and two teenage negotiators, he makes his home in Bel Air, a suburb of Los Angeles. He enjoys politics, reading and sailing in that order.